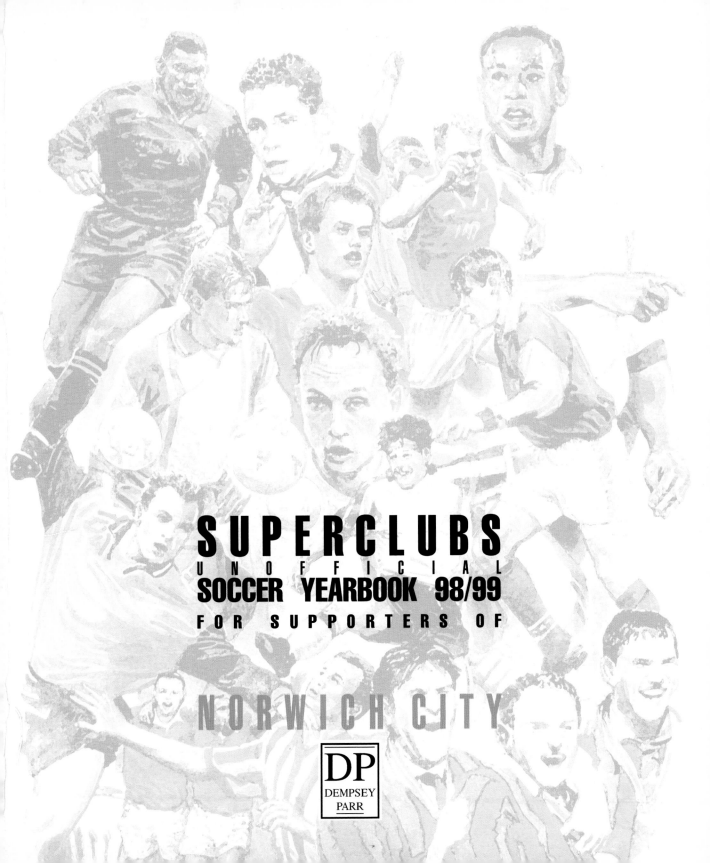

SUPERCLUBS
UNOFFICIAL
SOCCER YEARBOOK 98/99
FOR SUPPORTERS OF

NORWICH CITY

DP
DEMPSEY
PARR

First published in Great Britain in 1998 by
Dempsey Parr
13 Whiteladies Road
Clifton
Bristol BS8 1PB

ISBN: 1840841214

Produced for Dempsey Parr by
Prima Creative Services

Editorial director Roger Kean
Managing editor Tim Smith (Content E.D.B.)
Contributing authors
Steve Bradley
Jim Drewett (Deadline Features)
Steve Farragher
Sam Johnstone
Alex Leith (Deadline Features)
Rex Nash
Russell Smith
Tim Smith

Cover background and illustrations by Oliver Frey

Design and repro by Prima Creative Services

Printed and bound in Italy by L.E.G.O., Vicenza

Picture Acknowledgements
The publisher would like to thank the staff of Allsport and Action Images for their unstinting help and all the other libraries, newspapers and photographers who have made this edition possible. All pictures are credited alongside the photograph.

ALLSPORT: A GREAT CANARIES MOMENT – JEREMY GOSS CELEBRATES HIS GOAL IN THEIR 2–1 DEFEAT OF BAYERN MUNICH IN THE 1993-94 UEFA CUP

SUPERCLUBS
UNOFFICIAL
SOCCER YEARBOOK 98/99
FOR SUPPORTERS OF

NORWICH CITY

C O N T E N T S

STATISTICS

MAIN: NORWICH EVENING NEWS; INSET: NORWICH EVENIG POST

Close to being inaugural Premiership champions in 1993, Norwich's decline in recent seasons has made painful viewing for the Carrow Road faithful. Still, results haven't been quite as bad as the two-year run in the late 1970s when The Canaries went a club record 41 games without an away win. Around the same time, in the 1978–79 season, Norwich also set a football league record by drawing 23 of their 42 matches.

NORWICH EVENING NEWS

Date Formed: 1902
Date Entered Football League: 1920
Former Names: None
Official Nickname: The Canaries
Other Nicknames: None

MANAGERS SINCE JOINED LEAGUE:

Major Frank Buckley	(1919–20)	Archie Macauley	(1957–61)
Charles O'Hagan	(1920–21)	Willie Reid	(1961–62)
Albert Gosnell	(1921–26)	George Swindin	(1962)
Bert Stansfield	(1926)	Ron Ashman	(1962–66)
Cecil Potter	(1926–29)	Lol Morgan	(1966–69)
James Kerr	(1929–33)	Ron Saunders	(1969–73)
Tom Parker	(1933–37)	John Bond	(1973–80)
Bob Young	(1937–39)	Ken Brown	(1980–87)
Jimmy Jewell	(1939)	Dave Stringer	(1987–92)
Bob Young	(1939–45)	Mike Walker	(1992–94)
Cyril Spiers	(1946–47)	John Deehan	(1994–95)
Duggie Lochead	(1947–50)	Martin O'Neill	(1995)
Norman Low	(1950–55)	Gary Megson	(1995–96)
Tom Parker	(1955–57)	Mike Walker	(1996–98)

The Canaries may be able to fly, but 1997–98 brought some terrible disasters such as the 5–0 thrashing from Ipswich. Mind, they gave back as good against Huddersfield to guarantee staying in the First Division. Now Mike Walker (inset) has to try to better that 15th placing

CLUB HONOURS

Division Two Champions
    1972, 1986
Division Three Runners-Up
    1960
Division Three (South) Champions
    1934
Football League Cup Winners 1962
    (April 26th, Spotland) (First Leg)
    Norwich City v Rochdale 3–0; Scorers: Lythgoe (2) Punton
    (May 1st, Carrow Road) (Second Leg)
    Norwich City v Rochdale 1–0 ; Scorer: Hill

ACTION IMAGES

Football League Cup Winners 1985 (March 24th, Wembley)
    Norwich City v Sunderland 1–0
    Scorer: Chisholm (own goal)
Football League Cup Runners-Up 1973 (March 3rd, Wembley)
    Norwich City v Tottenham Hotspur 0–1
Football League Cup Runners-Up 1975 (March 1st, Wembley)
    Norwich City v Aston Villa 0–1

Chairman: Barry Lockwood
Club Sponsors: Colman's of Norwich

Record Attendance: 43,984 against Leicester City, FA Cup
    Sixth Round, March 30th 1963

Darren Eadie gives Canaries supporters consolation in scoring against Ipswich in the 2–0 defeat of their rivals, 26/9/97

Stadiums: 1902–1908 Newmarket Road
1908–1935 The Nest, Rosary Road
1935– Carrow Road
Address: Carrow Road, Norwich NR1 1JE
Capacity: 21,994
Stands: City Stand, Barclay Stand, River End
Stand, South Stand
Prices: Grade A Adults £17, £18, £20, £23
OAPs/Unemployed/Students £11
Children (U16) £5; Children (U12) £4, £1
Grade B Adults £11, £12, £14, £15, £17
OAPs/Unemployed/Students £6, £7
Children (U16) £3; Children (U12) £3, £1
Grade C Adults £4, £5
OAPs/Unemployed/Students £1
Children (U16) £1
Season ticket prices: Adults £205–£320
Senior Citizens £120–£320; Children £17–£320
Parking facilities: Multistorey car parks in town
centre and numerous spaces for street parking.

Preferred team formation: 4–4–2
Biggest rivals: Ipswich Town

BEST PUB

Kingsway, Carrow Rd – the only pub within 100 yds of the ground and always full of supporters on matchdays.

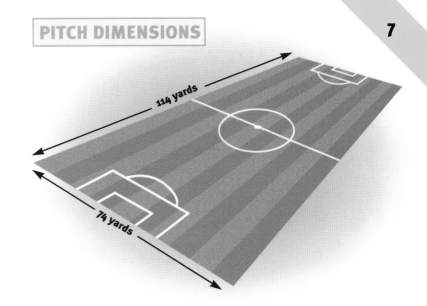
PITCH DIMENSIONS
114 yards
74 yards

Daryl Sutch takes on former Ipswich Town favourite Ian Marshall (now at Leicester City)

NORWICH EVENING NEWS

Programme: Official matchday programme
Programme Editor: Kevan Platt
Programme Price: £1.80
Bus routes to stadium: Norwich Railway Station ten minutes from Carrow Road. Bus Nos 12 and 14 from Norwich centre to ground.

FANZINES

Liverpool Are On The Tele Again!, 77 Pennyroyal, Old Catton, Norwich NR6 6JH
Ferry Cross The Wensum, 20 Chandlers Close, Wymondham, Norfolk NR6 6JN
I Can Drive A Tractor!, Darren Alcok, Melrose, Beccles Road, Great Yarmouth, NR31 9DJ
Cheep Shot, 17 Southerwood, Catton, Norwich NR6 6JN
Love Shag, Stacey Lodge, Flordon Road, Newton NR15 1QX

CONTACT NUMBERS

(Tel Code 01603)
● Main number 760 760
● Fax 613 886
● Ticket Office 761 661
● Club shop 218711
● Matchday info 760 760
● Clubcall 0891 121 144

LEADING PLAYERS

Keith Scott out-paces Sheffield United's Dean Saunders

1997/98 SEASON TOP 10 GOALSCORERS

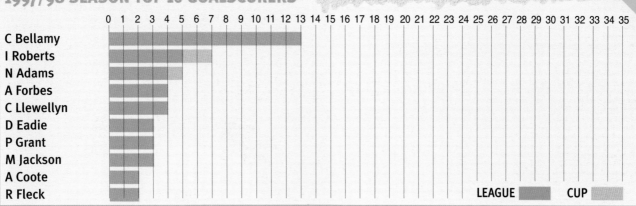

Chart — Top 10 goalscorers (scale 0–35):
- C Bellamy: 13 (LEAGUE)
- I Roberts: approx 5 (LEAGUE + CUP)
- N Adams: approx 5
- A Forbes: approx 4
- C Llewellyn: approx 4
- D Eadie: approx 3
- P Grant: approx 3
- M Jackson: approx 3
- A Coote: approx 2
- R Fleck: approx 2

LEAGUE | CUP

MOST LEAGUE APPEARANCES

PLAYER	APPEARANCES	SUBSTITUTE	GOALS
Andy Marshall	42	0	0
Matt Jackson	39	2	3
Daryl Sutch	40	0	1
Craig Bellam	30	6	13
Peter Grant	33	2	3
Adrian Forbes	28	5	4
Iwan Robert	2	2	5
Neil Adams	30	0	4
Robert Fleck	23	4	2
Victor Segura	22	3	0
Erik Fuglestad	23	1	2
Kevin Scott	22	2	0
Adrian Coote	11	12	2
Craig Fleming	20	2	1
Mike Milligan	20	0	0
Danny Mills	11	9	0
Darren Eadie	18	1	3
Christopher LLewellyn	10	5	4
Rob Newman	10	5	0
Shaun Carey	11	3	0

PLAYER STATISTICS

Record transfer fee paid:
Jon Newsome – £1,000,000 from Leeds United, June 1994

Record transfer fee received:
Chris Sutton – £5,000,000 from Blackburn Rovers, July 1994

Oldest player: Albert Sturgess, 42 years and 249 days against Millwall Athletic, February 14th 1925

Youngest player: Ian Davies, 17 years and 29 days against Birmingham City, April 27th 1974

International captains:
Martin O'Neill (Northern Ireland)

Most capped player:
Mark Bowen, 35, Wales (1988–1996)

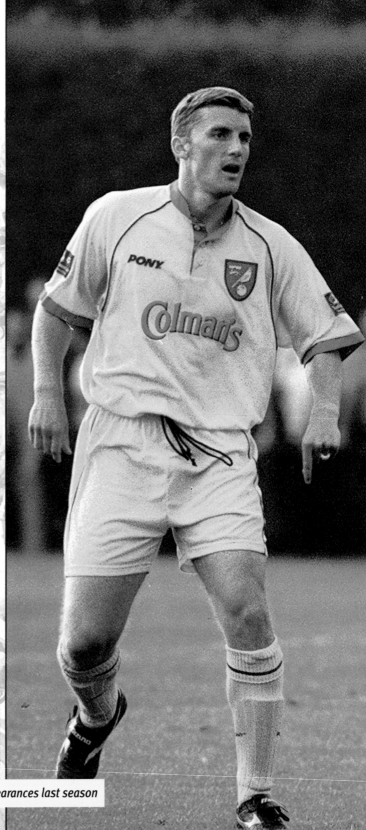

ANDREW MARSHALL

DOB: 14/4/75
Position: Goalkeeper
Usual shirt number: 1
Joined club: July 1993 from trainee
League Games played: 73
League Goals scored: 0
International caps: 0
League Debut: 27/12/94 v Nottingham Forest (A)

CRAIG FLEMING

DOB: 6/10/71
Position: Defender
Usual shirt number: 5
Joined club: June 1997 from Oldham Athletic
League Games played: 22
League Goals scored: 1
International caps: 0
League Debut: 9/8/97 v Wolverhampton Wanderers (H)

MATTHEW JACKSON

DOB: 19/10/71
Position: Defender
Usual shirt number: 6
Joined club: December 1996 from Everton
League Games played: 60
League Goals scored: 5
International caps: 0
League Debut: 26/12/97 v Queens Park Rangers (A)

JOHN POLSTON

DOB: 10/6/68
Position: Defender
Usual shirt number: 6
Joined club: July 1990 from Tottenham Hotspur
League Games played: 215
League Goals scored: 8
International caps: 0
League Debut: 25/8/90 v Sunderland (H)

NORWICH EVENING NEWS

Defender Matt Jackson scored three league goals in 39 appearances last season

Neale Fenn dampens the party spirit at Reading's final game at Elm Park last season

KEVIN SCOTT

DOB: 17/12/66
Position: Defender
Usual shirt number: 5
Joined club: January 1997 from Tottenham Hotspur
League Games played: 33
League Goals scored: 0
International caps: 0
League Debut: 22/1/97 v Stoke City (A)

VICTOR SEGURA

DOB: 30/3/73
Position: Defender
Usual shirt number: 3
Joined club: August 1997 from Ileida
League Games played: 25
League Goals scored: 0
International caps: 0
League Debut: 9/8/97 v Wolverhampton Wanderers (H)

DARYL SUTCH

DOB: 11/9/71
Position: Defender
Usual shirt number: 2
Joined club: July 1990 from trainee
League Games played: 165
League Goals scored: 7
International caps: 0
League Debut: 26/12/90 v Manchester United (A)

NEIL ADAMS

DOB: 23/11/65
Position: Midfielder
Usual shirt number: 7
Joined club: February 1994 from Oldham Athletic
League Games played: 164
League Goals scored: 22
International caps: 0
League Debut: 19/2/94 v Swindon Town (A)

NORWICH EVENING NEWS

ADRIAN COOTE

DOB: 30/9/78
Position: Midfielder
Usual shirt number: 8
Joined club: July 1997 from trainee
League Games played: 23
League Goals scored: 2
International caps: 0
League Debut: 13/9/97 v Port Vale (H)

DARREN EADIE

DOB: 10/6/75
Position: Midfielder
Usual shirt number: 11
Joined club: February 1993 from trainee
League Games played: 133
League Goals scored: 31
International caps: 0
League Debut: 18/9/93 v Queens Park Rangers (A)

CRAIG BELLAMY

DOB: 13/7/79
Position: Midfielder
Usual shirt number: 10
Joined club: January 1997 from trainee
League Games played: 39
League Goals scored: 13
International caps: 0
League Debut: 15/3/97 v Crystal Palace (A)

ADRIAN FORBES

DOB: 23/1/79
Position: Midfielder
Usual shirt number: 7
Joined club: January 1997 from trainee
League Games played: 53
League Goals scored: 4
International caps: 0
League Debut: 31/8/96 v Wolverhampton Wanderers (H)

SHAUN CAREY

DOB: 13/5/76
Position: Midfielder
Usual shirt number: 10
Joined club: July 1994 from trainee
League Games played: 37
League Goals scored: 0
International caps: 0
League Debut: 21/11/95 v West Bromwich Albion (A)

ERIK FUGLESTAD

DOB: 13/8/74
Position: Midfielder
Usual shirt number: 11
Joined club: November 1997 from Viking Stavanger
League Games played: 24
League Goals scored: 2
International caps: 0
League Debut: 15/11/97 v Middlesbrough (H)

Midfielder Darren Eadie suffered a suspected cheekbone fracture after the victorious 5–0 win over Huddersfield at the end of last season

NORWICH EVENING NEWS

LEE MARSHALL

DOB: 1/8/75
Position: Midfielder
Usual shirt number: 2
Joined club: April 1997 from Stockport County
League Games played: 2
League Goals scored: 0
International caps: 0
League Debut: 1/11/97 v Bury (H)

MIKE MILLIGAN

DOB: 20/2/67
Position: Midfielder
Usual shirt number: 9
Joined club: June 1994 from Oldham Athletic
League Games played: 111
League Goals scored: 5
International caps: Republic of Ireland (1)
League Debut: 19/9/94 v Ipswich Town (A)

KEITH O'NEILL

DOB: 16/2/76
Position: Midfielder
Usual shirt number: 11
Joined club: July 1994 from trainee
League Games played: 55
League Goals scored: 8
International caps: Republic of Ireland (9)
League Debut: 2/11/94 v Southampton (A)

PETER GRANT

DOB: 30/8/65
Position: Midfielder
Usual shirt number: 4
Joined club: August 1997 from Celtic
League Games played: 35
League Goals scored: 3
International caps: 2, Scotland
League Debut: 23/8/97 v Crewe (H)

CHRISTOPHER LLEWELLYN

DOB: 29/8/75
Position: Midfielder
Usual shirt number: 9
Joined club: Feb 1997 from trainee
League Games played: 15
League Goals scored: 4
International caps: 0
League Debut: 10/1/98 v Wolves (A)

IWAN ROBERTS

DOB: 26/6/68
Position: Striker
Usual shirt number: 9
Joined club: July 1997 from Wolverhampton Wanderers
League Games played: 31
League Goals scored: 5
International caps: Wales (7)
League Debut: 9/8/97 v Wolverhampton Wanderers (H)

ALL-TIME RECORDS

Team	Points	Goals	Position in Division One at start of 1998/99 season	Average position by points in the league since joining	Average position by goals in the league since joining
Barnsley	3965	5342	2	28	29
Birmingham City	4089	5655	7	22	23
Bolton Wanderers	4317	5995	1	11	15
Bradford City	3942	5258	13	3	12
Bristol City	4068	5270	23	23	31
Bury	4164	5738	17	20	21
Crewe Alexandra	3263	4482	11	64	56
Crystal Palace	3348	4310	3	59	65
Grimsby Town	4155	5791	24	21	20
Huddersfield Town	3672	4720	16	38	44
Ipswich Town	2693	3408	5	80	79
Norwich City	3272	4325	15	62	64
Oxford United	1850	2081	12	85	85
Portsmouth	3335	4497	20	31	38
Port Vale	3839	4984	19	60	55
QPR	3420	4515	21	52	54
Sheffield United	4309	6048	6	13	13
Stockport County	3967	5286	8	27	30
Sunderland	4384	6252	4	7	7
Swindon Town	3485	4626	18	45	47
Tranmere Rovers	3448	4716	14	49	45
Watford	3439	4479	22	50	57
West Bromwich	4286	6221	10	15	9
Wolverhampton	4414	6530	9	6	2

POINTS scale: 10 20 30 40 50 60 70 80 90 100 200 300 400 500

(3) Position in Division One at start of 1998/99 season

(92) Average position by points in the league since joining — includes 2 points for a win and 3 points for a win

(92) Average position by goals in the league since joining

1 Nottingham Forest (p)   5 Ipswich Town   9   Wolverhampton W   13 Bradford City   17 Bury   21 Queens Park Rangers
2 Middlesbrough (p)   6 Sheffield United   10 West Bromwich A   14 Tranmere Rovers   18 Swindon Town   22 Manchester City (r)
3 Sunderland   7 Birmingham City   11 Crewe Alexandra   15 Norwich City   19 Port Vale   23 Stoke City (r)
4 Charlton Athletic (p)   8 Stockport County   12 Oxford United   16 Huddersfield Town   20 Portsmouth   24 Reading (r)

Norwich City's total points since joining league **3272**

*Carrow Road: home
of Norwich City*
AEROFILMS

SUPERCLUBS
UNOFFICIAL
SOCCER YEARBOOK 98/99

JULY 1998 – JUNE 1999 DIARY
AND CLUB FIXTURES

Fixture dates are subject to change. FA Cup draws were not made at the time of
going to press. Worthington Cup draws are given where known at press time.

THE STORY OF DIVISION ONE SOCCER
IN THE 1997/98 SEASON

FOR SUPPORTERS OF
NORWICH CITY

DIVISION ONE CLUB ADDRESSES

BARNSLEY
Oakwell Ground, Grove Street, Barnsley, South Yorkshire, S71 1ET
Main No: 01266 211211

BIRMINGHAM CITY
St Andrews, Birmingham, B9 4NH
Main No: 0121 772 0101

BOLTON WANDERERS
The Reebok Stadium, Burnden Way, Lostock, Bolton, BL6 6JW
Main No: 01204 389 200

BRADFORD CITY
The Pulse Stadium, Valley Parade, Bradford, West Yorkshire, BD8 7DY
Main No: 01274 773355

BRISTOL CITY
Ashton Gate, Bristol, BS3 2EJ
Main No: 0117 963 0630

BURY
Gigg Lane, Bury, BL9 9HR
Main No: 0161 764 4881

CREWE ALEXANDRA
Gresty Road, Crewe, Cheshire, CW2 6EB
Main No: 01270 213014

CRYSTAL PALACE
Selhurst Park, London, SE25 6PU
Main No: 0181 768 6000

GRIMSBY TOWN
Blundell Park, Cleethorpes, North East Lincolnshire, DN35 7PY
Main No: 01472 697 111

HUDDERSFIELD TOWN
The Alfred McAlpine Stadium, Huddersfield, West Yorkshire, HD1 6PX
Main No: 01484 420 335

IPSWICH TOWN
Portman Road, Ipswich, Suffolk, IP1 2DA
Main No: 01473 400 500

NORWICH CITY
Carrow Road, Norwich, NR1 1JE
Main No: 01603 760 760

OXFORD UNITED
Manor Ground, Headington, Oxford, Oxfordshire, OX3 7RS
Main No: 01865 761 503

PORTSMOUTH
Frogmore Road. Portsmouth, PO4 8RA
Main No: 01705 731 204

PORT VALE
Vale Park, Burslem, Stoke-on-Trent, ST6 1AW
Main No: 01782 814 134

QUEENS PARK RANGERS
Rangers Stadium, South Africa Road, London, W12 7PA
Main No: 0181 743 0262

SHEFFIELD UNITED
Bramall Lane Ground, Sheffield, S2 4SU
Main No: 0114 221 5757

STOCKPORT COUNTY
Edgeley Park, Hardcastle Road, Stockport, Cheshire, SK3 9DD
Main No: 0161 286 8888

SUNDERLAND
Sunderland Stadium of Light, Sunderland, SR5 1SU
Main No: 0191 551 5000

SWINDON TOWN
County Ground, Swindon, Wiltshire, SN1 2ED
Main No: 01793 430 430

TRANMERE ROVERS
Prenton Park, Prenton Park West, Birkenhead, L42 9PN
Main No: 0151 608 4194

WATFORD
Vicarage Road Stadium, Watford, WD1 8ER
Main No: 01923 496 000

WEST BROMWICH ALBION
The Hawthorns, West Bromwich B71 4LF
Main No: 0121 525 8888

WOLVERHAMPTON WANDERERS
Molineux Ground, Wolverhampton, WV1 4QR
Main No: 01902 655 00

ALL-CLUB LOCATIONS

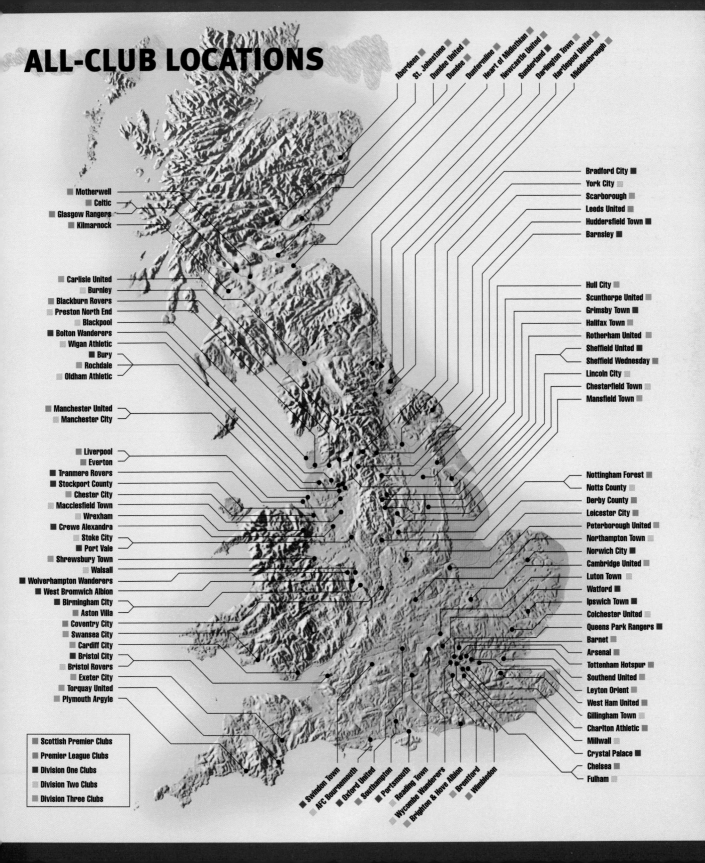

Aberdeen
St. Johnstone
Dundee United
Dundee
Dunfermline
Heart of Midlothian
Newcastle United
Sunderland
Darlington Town
Hartlepool United
Middlesbrough

Bradford City ■
York City ■
Scarborough ■
Leeds United ■
Huddersfield Town ■
Barnsley ■

Hull City ■
Scunthorpe United ■
Grimsby Town ■
Halifax Town ■
Rotherham United ■
Sheffield United ■
Sheffield Wednesday ■
Lincoln City ■
Chesterfield Town ■
Mansfield Town ■

Nottingham Forest ■
Notts County ■
Derby County ■
Leicester City ■
Peterborough United ■
Northampton Town ■
Norwich City ■
Cambridge United ■
Luton Town ■
Watford ■
Ipswich Town ■
Colchester United ■
Queens Park Rangers ■
Barnet ■
Arsenal ■
Tottenham Hotspur ■
Southend United ■
Leyton Orient ■
West Ham United ■
Gillingham Town ■
Charlton Athletic ■
Millwall ■
Crystal Palace ■
Chelsea ■
Fulham ■

■ Motherwell
■ Celtic
■ Glasgow Rangers
■ Kilmarnock

■ Carlisle United
■ Burnley
■ Blackburn Rovers
■ Preston North End
■ Blackpool
■ Bolton Wanderers
■ Wigan Athletic
■ Bury
■ Rochdale
■ Oldham Athletic

■ Manchester United
■ Manchester City

■ Liverpool
■ Everton
■ Tranmere Rovers
■ Stockport County
■ Chester City
■ Macclesfield Town
■ Wrexham
■ Crewe Alexandra
■ Stoke City
■ Port Vale
■ Shrewsbury Town
■ Walsall
■ Wolverhampton Wanderers
■ West Bromwich Albion
■ Birmingham City
■ Aston Villa
■ Coventry City
■ Swansea City
■ Cardiff City
■ Bristol City
■ Bristol Rovers
■ Exeter City
■ Torquay United
■ Plymouth Argyle

Swindon Town
AFC Bournemouth
Oxford United
Southampton
Portsmouth
Reading Town
Wycombe Wanderers
Brighton & Hove Albion
Brentford
Wimbledon

■ Scottish Premier Clubs
■ Premier League Clubs
■ Division One Clubs
■ Division Two Clubs
■ Division Three Clubs

CALENDAR 1998

January
	M	T	W	T	F	S	S
1				1	2	3	4
2	5	6	7	8	9	10	11
3	12	13	14	15	16	17	18
4	19	20	21	22	23	24	25
5	26	27	28	29	30	31	

February
	M	T	W	T	F	S	S
5							1
6	2	3	4	5	6	7	8
7	9	10	11	12	13	14	15
8	16	17	18	19	20	21	22
9	23	24	25	26	27	28	

March
	M	T	W	T	F	S	S
9							1
10	2	3	4	5	6	7	8
11	9	10	11	12	13	14	15
12	16	17	18	19	20	21	22
13	23	24	25	26	27	28	29
14	30	31					

April
	M	T	W	T	F	S	S
14			1	2	3	4	5
15	6	7	8	9	10	11	12
16	13	14	15	16	17	18	19
17	20	21	22	23	24	25	26
18	27	28	29	30			

May
	M	T	W	T	F	S	S
18					1	2	3
19	4	5	6	7	8	9	10
20	11	12	13	14	15	16	17
21	18	19	20	21	22	23	24
22	25	26	27	28	29	30	31

June
	M	T	W	T	F	S	S
23	1	2	3	4	5	6	7
24	8	9	10	11	12	13	14
25	15	16	17	18	19	20	21
26	22	23	24	25	26	27	28
27	29	30					

July
	M	T	W	T	F	S	S
27			1	2	3	4	5
28	6	7	8	9	10	11	12
29	13	14	15	16	17	18	19
30	20	21	22	23	24	25	26
31	27	28	29	30	31		

August
	M	T	W	T	F	S	S
31						1	2
32	3	4	5	6	7	8	9
33	10	11	12	13	14	15	16
34	17	18	19	20	21	22	23
35	24	25	26	27	28	29	30
36	31						

September
	M	T	W	T	F	S	S
36		1	2	3	4	5	6
37	7	8	9	10	11	12	13
38	14	15	16	17	18	19	20
39	21	22	23	24	25	26	27
40	28	29	30				

October
	M	T	W	T	F	S	S
40				1	2	3	4
41	5	6	7	8	9	10	11
42	12	13	14	15	16	17	18
43	19	20	21	22	23	24	25
44	26	27	28	29	30	31	

November
	M	T	W	T	F	S	S
44							1
45	2	3	4	5	6	7	8
46	9	10	11	12	13	14	15
47	16	17	18	19	20	21	22
48	23	24	25	26	27	28	29
49	30						

December
	M	T	W	T	F	S	S
49		1	2	3	4	5	6
50	7	8	9	10	11	12	13
51	14	15	16	17	18	19	20
52	21	22	23	24	25	26	27
53	28	29	30	31			

UK Holiday   **Scotland Holiday**   N. Ireland Holiday   Not in Scotland

CALENDAR 1999

January

	M	T	W	T	F	S	S
1				1	2	3
2	4	5	6	7	8	9	10
3	11	12	13	14	15	16	17
4	18	19	20	21	22	23	24
5	25	26	27	28	29	30	31

February

	M	T	W	T	F	S	S
6	1	2	3	4	5	6	7
7	8	9	10	11	12	13	14
8	15	16	17	18	19	20	21
9	22	23	24	25	26	27	28

March

	M	T	W	T	F	S	S
10	1	2	3	4	5	6	7
11	8	9	10	11	12	13	14
12	15	16	17	18	19	20	21
13	22	23	24	25	26	27	28
14	29	30	31				

April

	M	T	W	T	F	S	S
14				1	2	3	4
15	5	6	7	8	9	10	11
16	12	13	14	15	16	17	18
17	19	20	21	22	23	24	25
18	26	27	28	29	30		

May

	M	T	W	T	F	S	S
18						1	2
19	3	4	5	6	7	8	9
20	10	11	12	13	14	15	16
21	17	18	19	20	21	22	23
22	24	25	26	27	28	29	30
23	31						

June

	M	T	W	T	F	S	S
23		1	2	3	4	5	6
24	7	8	9	10	11	12	13
25	14	15	16	17	18	19	20
26	21	22	23	24	25	26	27
27	28	29	30				

July

	M	T	W	T	F	S	S
27				1	2	3	4
28	5	6	7	8	9	10	11
29	12	13	14	15	16	17	18
30	19	20	21	22	23	24	25
31	26	27	28	29	30	31	

August

	M	T	W	T	F	S	S
31							1
32	2	3	4	5	6	7	8
33	9	10	11	12	13	14	15
34	16	17	18	19	20	21	22
35	23	24	25	26	27	28	29
36	30	31					

September

	M	T	W	T	F	S	S
36			1	2	3	4	5
37	6	7	8	9	10	11	12
38	13	14	15	16	17	18	19
39	20	21	22	23	24	25	26
40	27	28	29	30			

October

	M	T	W	T	F	S	S
40				1	2	3
41	4	5	6	7	8	9	10
42	11	12	13	14	15	16	17
43	18	19	20	21	22	23	24
44	25	26	27	28	29	30	31

November

	M	T	W	T	F	S	S
45	1	2	3	4	5	6	7
46	8	9	10	11	12	13	14
47	15	16	17	18	19	20	21
48	22	23	24	25	26	27	28
49	29	30					

December

	M	T	W	T	F	S	S
49		1	2	3	4	5
50	6	7	8	9	10	11	12
51	13	14	15	16	17	18	19
52	20	21	22	23	24	25	26
53	27	28	29	30	31		

Monday June 29 1998

Tuesday June 30 1998

Wednesday July 1 1998

Thursday July 2 1998

Friday July 3 1998

Saturday July 4 1998   Sunday July 5 1998

Monday July 6 1998

Tuesday July 7 1998

Wednesday July 8 1998

Thursday July 9 1998

Friday July 10 1998

Saturday July 11 1998   Sunday July 12 1998

 9 August, 1997: the opening day's biggest gate was at Maine Road where 30,000 fans were treated to an impromptu Oasis walkabout before kick-off. Despite allegations of rude gestures from the pop duo, the game was a well-humoured event and the honours were shared in a 2–2 draw. Ex-Pompey lad Lee Bradbury, who had recently joined Man City in a club record £3 million transfer deal was man-marked out of the match by his old teammates but two other debutantes had better games; Dutchman Gerard Wiekens scoring for City, while Aussie John Aloisi netted for Pompey.

ALLSPORT

Don't look back in anguish:
Noel Gallacher on walkabout

'I can't wait for the rest of the season,' was Birmingham City Manager Trevor Francis' comment after watching his side cruise to victory over Stoke. Last season's leading scorer for Birmingham, Paul Devlin, opened their account after 33 minutes with a header. But the game was stolen by his new striking partner, Peter Ndlovu, who scored from close range with just three minutes to play to make the score 2–0. 'He was always elusive, always a danger and there were moments of sheer brilliance,' said a delighted Francis of the man he had just signed for £1.6 million from Coventry City.

On the ball:
Brian Deane of
Sheffield United
tussles with
Sunderland's
Kevin Ball on
10/8/97

Monday July 13 1998

Tuesday July 14 1998

Wednesday July 15 1998

Thursday July 16 1998

Friday July 17 1998

Saturday July 18 1998   Sunday July 19 1998

Monday July 20 1998

Tuesday July 21 1998

Wednesday July 22 1998

Thursday July 23 1998

Friday July 24 1998

Saturday July 25 1998   Sunday July 26 1998

 Manchester City may be able to boast famous names among the attractions for a visit to Maine Road, but Sunderland's brand new Stadium of Light managed to upstage the older ground with a 39,000 strong crowd for its first ever match on 15 August. On the pitch, too, Sunderland were more than a match for their opponents, winning the game 3–1 despite a spirited performance from Martyn Margetson in the City goal who denied former City idol Niall Quinn's marvellous header. However, the wily Quinn marked his first anniversary at Sunderland with the Stadium of Light's first goal by latching onto an errant backpass from hapless Tony Vaughan after just 17 minutes.

ACTION IMAGES

Georgiou Kinkladze got the only one back against Sunderland

 There have been many 'supersubs' in the past, but in their 3–2 victory over Crewe Alexandra on 16 August, one West Bromwich Albion player redefined the term. After coming on in the 56th minute, when WBA were 2–1 down, Lee Hughes scored two superb goals to win Albion the game. Hughes, signed from Kidderminster in the summer, is a lifelong Albion fan, whose only dream has been to play for the Baggies. While there was jubilation in the Albion camp, Crewe Manager Dario Gradi was despondent: 'I can't see this team winning. One or two have been found out at this level,' he told the post-match press conference.

Dele Adebola of Crewe, watched by managers with money and a need for a classy striker

Monday July 27 1998

Tuesday July 28 1998

Wednesday July 29 1998

Thursday July 30 1998

Friday July 31 1998

Saturday August 1 1998

Sunday August 2 1998

Monday August 3 1998

Tuesday August 4 1998

Wednesday August 5 1998

Thursday August 6 1998

Friday August 7 1998

Saturday August 8 1998
Crewe Alexandra at Norwich City

Sunday August 9 1998

 It was a fittingly miserable end to the dream... Fabrizio Ravanelli's last game for Middlesbrough turned out to be a dreary affair for him. Stranded alone up front Rav looked as forlornly out of place as an Italian international star in a struggling First Division side should. It wasn't much better for the rest of the Middlesbrough squad. Kept out of the game by a couple of brilliant saves from Stoke goalkeeper Carl Muggleton, Boro eventually went down 1–0 at home to a 60th minute strike from Paul Stewart, a player who, in stark contrast to the £7-million-Ravanelli, had joined Stoke on a free transfer from Sunderland in the close season.

August saw another home win for Birmingham City

 On 23 August, Birmingham City confirmed they were a team to be reckoned with in the First Division by beating Reading in a convincing 3–0 performance that earned them maximum points from their opening two games. The Blues fans were particularly delighted with the second goal, a header from Steve Bruce – the former Manchester United star's first for Birmingham. He had failed to score in 32 appearances the previous season. Paul Devlin and Peter Ndlovu supplied the other two goals in a rout of an out-classed Reading side who had Australian International Andy Bernal sent off in the 62nd minute.

Fabrizio Ravanelli's finally waved the white feather to the northeast in August 1997

Monday August 10 1998

Tuesday August 11 1998
Norwich City at Swansea City – Worthington Cup 1 (1)

Wednesday August 12 1998

Thursday August 13 1998

Friday August 14 1998

Saturday August 15 1998
Norwich City at Stockport County

Sunday August 16 1998

Monday August 17 1998

Tuesday August 18 1998
Swansea City at Norwich City – Worthington Cup 1 (2)

Wednesday August 19 1998

Thursday August 20 1998

Friday August 21 1998

Saturday August 22 1998
Queens Park Rangers at Norwich City

Sunday August 23 1998

Nottingham Forest's 4–0 demolition of Queens Park Rangers on 30 August gave them their best start to a season in 41 years, as it became four victories from four games. Dutch striker Pierre Van Hooijdonk scored a devastating hat-trick that left Rangers totally demoralised. His partnership with Dean Saunders tore Rangers' defence apart. Saunders scored the other goal and made two for Van Hooijdonk. A typically downbeat Dave Bassett, Forest's sole man in charge after Stuart Pearce's transfer to Newcastle United, said at the end of the match: 'We didn't get enough strikes at goal in the first half. I thought we fiddled too much.'

ALLSPORT

Scott Gemill, promotion and a World Cup place in the same year

On a day when a perennial Wolves favourite, Steve Bull, rediscovered his scoring habit after an 11-game drought, his new young partner upstaged him. Robbie Keane, a 17-year-old Dubliner and Republic of Ireland youth international, scored two brilliant goals to reassure the Wolves fans that there would be life after Bull. A thrilling home match against newly promoted Bury finished 4–2 after an incredible 86th minute strike from the young Keane, hit from 20 yards out. 'It was a great finish by Robbie. He's a terrific prospect,' enthused the clearly delighted Wolves manager, Mark McGhee.

Tony Battersby's goal – not enough to stop Wolves burying Bury 4–2

Edinho – Bradford's Ronaldo
look-alike having fun

ALLSPORT

Newly promoted Bradford City and their fans took great delight in beating old foes Huddersfield 2–1 on 2 September, especially as it happened at Huddersfield's award-winning Alfred McAlpine stadium. Edinho proved again that there is a place for talented Brazilians in English League football as he scored one and made one in a virtuoso display of passing and moving football. He exchanged long passes with Peter Beagrie for his goal and crossed the ball in for Robbie Blakes. The Terriers' consolation came in the 75th minute when Bristol Rover's old boy Marcus Stewart seized on a knock-out from Bradford keeper, Robert Zabica.

After a shaky start to the season, Peter Reid's Sunderland were beginning to show the form they were capable of as they beat Bradford 0–4 in a scintillating display of football on 5 September. This was Bradford's second match in three days, but not even that could explain the way Sunderland entirely dominated this game, which culminated in a three-goal flurry in six minutes of the first half. Sunderland were without the injured Niall Quinn, but the lack of a front man just seemed to encourage them all to try to get on the score-sheet. The goals came from Michael Gray, Lee Clark, Kevin Phillips and Allan Johnston.

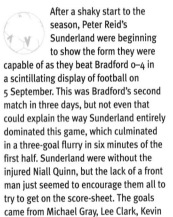

*Oxford crimps Wolves'
season as they slap
them 3–0 in September*

QUIZ 1 ABOUT NORWICH CITY

1 Which former Canaries player holds the record for the fastest Premiership goal scored by a substitute?
 a) Chris Sutton
 b) Jamie Cureton ✓
 c) Ruel Fox

2 How much did Rangers pay Norwich for Chris Woods?
 a) £1.25m
 b) £1m ✗ b
 c) £750,000

3 Shaun Carey has been capped at Under-21 level for which country?
 a) Northern Ireland
 b) Republic Of Ireland ✗ A
 c) Wales

ALLSPORT

4 What position on the field did Mike Walker occupy when he was a player?
 a) Goal
 b) Central defence ✗ A
 c) Central midfield

5 Who beat the Canaries 1–0 in the semi-finals of the FA Cup in 1989?
 a) Everton
 b) Liverpool ✓
 c) Arsenal

6 After being relegated to the Second Division at the end of the 1973-74 season, Norwich bounced straight back up as runners-up behind which club?
 a) Ipswich Town
 b) Manchester United ✗ B
 c) Coventry City

7 From which club did Norwich City sign goalkeeper Bryan Gunn in October 1986?
 a) Aberdeen
 b) Hearts
 c) Motherwell ✓

8 How many times has Robert Fleck been capped by Scotland?
 a) 4
 b) 8
 c) 12 ✓

9 How many league appearances did former Liverpool star Jan Molby make for the Canaries?
 a) 3
 b) 5
 c) 7 ✗ A

10 What club-record did Norwich break in the 1995-96 season?
 a) 19 different players scored in senior matches
 b) 19 different players were booked ✓
 c) They drew 19 league games

Monday August 24 1998

Tuesday August 25 1998

Wednesday August 26 1998

Thursday August 27 1998

Friday August 28 1998

Saturday August 29 1998   Sunday August 30 1998
Norwich City at West Bromwich Albion

Monday August 31 1998
Bolton Wanderers at Norwich City

Tuesday September 1 1998

Wednesday September 2 1998

Thursday September 3 1998

Friday September 4 1998

Saturday September 5 1998   Sunday September 6 1998
Norwich City at Watford

13 September: Dave Bassett's first return to Bramall lane in two years was a bittersweet homecoming. The now Nottingham Forest Coach had left Sheffield United under a cloud two years before, but he was treated to a warm reception from the Blades fans, who presented him with a silver tankard before kick-off. Forest, flying high at the top of the league, dominated the game and created chance after chance, but a single strike from Gareth Taylor, a player sacked by Basset when he was at Crystal Palace, gave the home side all three points. At least Bassett had something to drown his sorrows in.

ACTION IMAGES

Andy Townsend – Boro's quiet achiever

The Molineux crowd jeered their manager, Mark McGhee, before the start of their home tie against Charlton Athletic. And their doubts were not entirely dispelled even though Wolves went on to a 3–1 victory, topped by two goals for Steve Bull and a 25-yard effort from Steve Froggatt. Although the score looked one-sided, the match was anything but, with Charlton having lots of possession, but just failing to turn it into goals. The obviously relieved McGhee said after the match: 'I would put my house on us winning promotion. Everything is coming into place and I am very optimistic.'

Mixing it: Anthony Barness and Mixu Paatelainen tackle for the ball on 13/9/97

Monday September 7 1998

Tuesday September 8 1998
Norwich City at Barnsley

Wednesday September 9 1998

Thursday September 10 1998

Friday September 11 1998

Saturday September 12 1998
Bury at Norwich City

Sunday September 13 1998

Monday September 14 1998

Tuesday September 15 1998

Wednesday September 16 1998

Thursday September 17 1998

Friday September 18 1998

Saturday September 19 1998
Norwich City at Sheffield United

Sunday September 20 1998

'It was a great team performance, all I did was finish some excellent teamwork,' was Canadian International Paul Peschisolido's modest summing up of his hat-trick for West Bromwich Albion as they won 3–1 away at Bury on 27 September. The evenly spaced goals in the 10th, 45th and 61st minutes were a testament to his consistent form throughout the match and came on top of two goals in his previous match. Peschisolido, in contract talks with Albion added 'I don't want to go. If we keep creating chances and accepting them we will be there or thereabouts next May.'

ACTION IMAGES

Bradford's Jamie Lawrence couldn't stop Charlton's four-goal slaughter

Two of the top runners for the Division One championship, Manchester City and Swindon Town met at Maine Road for a six-goal Saturday thriller that same day. Unfortunately for Swindon, it was all one-way traffic. Georgiou Kinkladze, fresh from World Cup duty for Georgia in midweek, started the ball rolling with a glorious 30-yard goal from a free kick after just seven minutes. For the rest of the match he seemed to mesmerise the Swindon defenders, and was instrumental in Manchester City's victory. Paul Dickov played a major part as well, scoring two and making another.

Another Kinky run for Manchester City

Monday September 21 1998

Tuesday September 22 1998

Wednesday September 23 1998

Thursday September 24 1998

Friday September 25 1998

Saturday September 26 1998
Birmingham City at Norwich City

Sunday September 27 1998

Monday September 28 1998

Tuesday September 29 1998
Sunderland at Norwich City

Wednesday September 30 1998

Thursday October 1 1998

Friday October 2 1998

Saturday October 3 1998
Norwich City at Port Vale

Sunday October 4 1998

---

3 October: Colin Cooper couldn't get a first-team game at Nottingham Forest at the start of the season, despite being club captain and a City Ground stalwart. The papers said he'd fallen out with boss Dave Bassett, and was reported to be on his way to West Ham for £2.5 million. But, back in the side after weeks out, he scored the first goal of this 2–0 away victory. Forest were now clear by four points at the top of the table with poor Huddersfield stranded firmly at the bottom. Huddersfield manager Brian Horton was sacked the day after.

ACTION IMAGES

Colin Cooper eyes the prize as Forest's march to the Title picks up

After five years in charge at The Valley, Charlton Athletic's highly-regarded manager Alan Curbishley celebrated with a superb 4–2 away win over Queen's Park Rangers. Incredibly this was Charlton's third four-goal victory in only nine games and moved them to within striking distance of the top of the table. 'Over recent years, the reason we haven't got promotion is that we haven't scored enough goals,' Curbishley said. 'Now we've got Clive Mendonca and Steve Jones scoring and the rest of the team have responded.'

Stoke City kept their heads above water with a 2–1 victory over neighbouring Port Vale

Monday October 5 1998

Tuesday October 6 1998

Wednesday October 7 1998

Thursday October 8 1998

Friday October 9 1998

Saturday October 10 1998
Grimsby Town at Norwich City

Sunday October 11 1998

Monday October 12 1998

Tuesday October 13 1998

Wednesday October 14 1998

Thursday October 15 1998

Friday October 16 1998

Saturday October 17 1998
Norwich City at Crystal Palace

Sunday October 18 1998

'We're getting nose-bleeds because we're so high up the table,' was the verdict of West Bromwich Albion's Paul Hunt after another victory, this time 3–2 away against Portsmouth on 18 October. Hunt scored two of his team's three goals to make up for the disappointment of missing out on his team's midweek Coca-Cola cup tie with Liverpool, but his efforts were overshadowed by teammate Paul Mardon's spectacular overhead strike early in the match. Portsmouth were unlucky to come away from the match with no points after a late surge brought them back from 3–0 down, with goals by Foster and McLoughlin.

ALLSPORT

Port Vale's Paul Musslewhite looks on in anguish

The first Potteries' derby in Stoke City's new Britannia stadium, on 12 October, was a classic of its kind, with goals, missed chances and two controversial decisions adding to the excitement as Stoke beat Port Vale 2–1. Kevin Keen set up Richard Forsyth for Stoke's first goal and also scored the winner. Forsyth could have had more, particularly a 16th minute chance that was hauled back over the line by Port Vale keeper Paul Musselwhite. The officials waved 'play on', though it looked clearly a goal. Later in the match Stoke defender Steve Tweed appeared to handball in the penalty area, but no penalty was given. Tony Naylor got Port Vale's consolation goal.

Richard Sneekes tries to beat Liverpool's Bjornebye as the Baggies crash in the Coca-Cola Cup

Mike Sheron of QPR helps take Manchester City down 2–0 at Loftus Road

On 18 October, Swindon's great start to the season foundered on the rock of Wolverhampton Wanderers' resolve in an ugly game that had a tally of three sending-offs and four bookings by its bitter end. Steve Bull was dismissed for Wolves, still one shy of his 300th league goal for the club. But that was nothing compared to poor Swindon, who lost two men, playing out the last 20 minutes with only nine on the pitch. Up until that point it had been an even game, with the score 1–1. But Keith Curle and Paul Simpson, on loan to Wolves from Derby, settled the match 3–1 with two late goals.

Swindon's Mark Robinson fights Bury's Andy Gray for the ball, 11/10/97

24 October: it should have been Forest's game, but after on-loan keeper Dave Beasant was sent off for a challenge on Martin Williams in the 55th minute, home-team Reading came back strongly to get a point from a game that finished 3–3. Beasant's dismissal lead to defender Steve Chettle having a torrid time in the Forest goal, but despite the setback this was a good game for Forest. Two goals from the on-form Van Hooijdonk, and the return of injury-beset England international Steve Stone were, however, pointers to a rosier future for Forest. And the result ensured that they stayed two points clear at the top with a game in hand over their nearest rivals.

ALLSPORT

ALLSPORT

QUIZ 2 REFEREE QUIZ

1 In the event of the crossbar being broken, or somehow moved from its position, and replacing it is not possible, the referee will:
   a) Allow another item such as a taut rope to be used as a replacement.
   b) Allow play to continue without a crossbar
   c) Abandon the game.

2 The minimum height for a corner flagpole is
   a) 1.5m
   b) .5m
   c) 1.75m

3 A goal is scored from a throw-in. Does the referee:
   a) Disallow it?
   b) Use his discretion?
   c) Allow the goal?

4 Only eight players appear for one side in a professional eleven-a-side game. Does the referee:
   a) Abandon the game?
   b) Allow the game to continue?
   c) Allow non-registered players to fill-in and continue the game?

5 An outfield player swaps positions with the goalkeeper without informing the referee. The ref notices while the ball is in play. Does he?
   a) Immediately send both players off?
   b) Allow play to continue and wait for a natural break?
   c) Immediately book both players?

6 The ref gives a direct free kick in your penalty area. One of your players kicks it back to the keeper who misses the ball completely. The ball goes into your own net! Does the referee:
   a) Order the free kick to be taken again?
   b) Award a goal to the opposition?
   c) Award a corner-kick to the opposition?

7 What is wrong with the picture at the top of a penalty shoot-out?
   a) The goalkeeper of the team taking the kick is in the centre circle with the rest of his teammates. Should he be standing on the 18-yard line?
   b) The goalkeeper has his arms raised when they should be still and by his side?
   c) The referee is in the penalty area causing a distraction when he should be standing on the 18-yard line.

8 There are three minutes left in a game when one manager decides to make a substitution. Two minutes later the ball goes out of play, it takes one minute to make the substitution. Does the referee:
   a) Blow the whistle for full-time when the player enters the field?
   b) Book the manager for time-wasting?
   c) Add time on for the substitution?

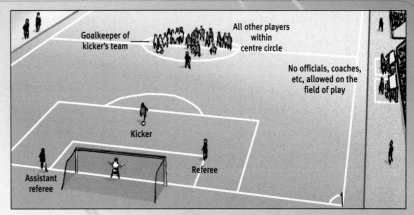

Goalkeeper of kicker's team — All other players within centre circle — No officials, coaches, etc, allowed on the field of play — Kicker — Assistant referee — Referee

9 What is wrong with this picture of the 'Technical Area'?

   a) Nothing.
   b) There are no markings showing the correct distance.
   c) The distances shown are wrong.

10 In this picture, does the referee:
   a) Give the goal?
   b) Not give the goal?
   c) Give a drop-ball?

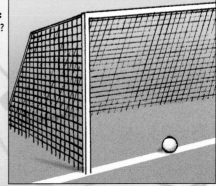

Answers: 1.c 2.a 3.a 4.b 5.b 6.c 7.a 8.c 9.a 10.b

Monday October 19 1998

Tuesday October 20 1998
Norwich City at Ipswich Town

Wednesday October 21 1998

Thursday October 22 1998

Friday October 23 1998

Saturday October 24 1998
Huddersfield Town at Norwich City

Sunday October 25 1998

Monday October 26 1998

Tuesday October 27 1998

Wednesday October 28 1998

Thursday October 29 1998

Friday October 30 1998

Saturday October 31 1998
Norwich City at Portsmouth

Sunday November 1 1998

Frank Clark was probably wishing he was still in charge at Nottingham Forest this week, after Manchester City were beaten 2–0 away at QPR on 25 October. At the post-match press conference he was even forced to come out with the chilling line, 'I have the full support of the chairman and the board.' After 10 months in charge, and having spent £9 million on his side, Clark's position in charge at Maine Road looked in jeopardy. To compound the misery of players and fans, Clark seemed to be blaming some of his players, saying: 'Sometimes when the ball goes into the box, I wonder if they really want it enough.'

Steve Morrow and Paul Dickou clash in QPR's 2–0 defeat of Man City

Ipswich Town were lifted out of the bottom three thanks to a spirited performance in a 2–2 draw against Sheffield United at Portman Road on 9 November. Goals for Brian Deane and Mitch Ward looked to have clinched a victory for The Blades, but Andy Legg, playing only his second game for Ipswich, pulled one back in the 50th minute and the scene was set for a dramatic climax. With midfielder Don Hutchison playing in goal for Sheffield after regular keeper Simon Tracey was carried off with concussion, Sheffield looked surprisingly comfortable. But then on came Ipswich substitute Neil Gregory to equalise with just three minutes left on the clock.

Neil Gregory's last-minute equaliser for Ipswich versus Sheffield United in November 1997

Monday November 2 1998

Tuesday November 3 1998

Wednesday November 4 1998

Thursday November 5 1998

Friday November 6 1998

Saturday November 7 1998

Bradford City at Norwich City

Sunday November 8 1998

Monday November 9 1998

Tuesday November 10 1998

Wednesday November 11 1998

Thursday November 12 1998

Friday November 13 1998

Saturday November 14 1998

Wolverhampton Wanderers at Norwich City   FA Cup round 1

Sunday November 15 1998

Huddersfield had been glued to the bottom of the First Division, but, on 1 November, a 3–1 home victory over Stoke City pulled them within striking distance of the other strugglers. Huddersfield went ahead just after half-time through Lee Richardson. In the 79th minute young Stoke defender Andrew Griffin equalised with his first goal for the club. But while Stoke were busy celebrating, Huddersfield's Marcus Stewart regained the lead. The icing on Huddersfield's cake came in the last minute of the match when Stoke keeper Muggleton, having come upfield for a corner, was left stranded, leaving Paul Dalton to score Huddersfield's third in an empty net.

Paul Dalton got Huddersfield's third goal, and offered the club hope

Wolves' Robbie Keane put his team ahead after 27 minutes in their home tie against Ipswich. But young Ipswich debutant, David Johnson, put the Town back on level footing before half-time, and the game ended 1–1. Johnson, signed from Bury for £1 million on the Thursday before the match, wasted no time in making an impression. Fellow Ipswich player, defender Paul Cundy, said: 'David is certainly a real keg of dynamite. He is going to make a tremendous impact on the team.' Johnson himself was a little more reticent, explaining: 'I think I'll be able to play a lot better when I learn the names of our players.'

Even a Delia Smith-inspired
Norwich couldn't stop
Paul Merson and Boro
dishing out a 3–1 victory

Monday November 16 1998

Tuesday November 17 1998

Wednesday November 18 1998

Thursday November 19 1998

Friday November 20 1998

Saturday November 21 1998
Norwich City at Tranmere Rovers

Sunday November 22 1998

Monday November 23 1998

Tuesday November 24 1998

Wednesday November 25 1998

Thursday November 26 1998

Friday November 27 1998

Saturday November 28 1998
Oxford United at Norwich City

Sunday November 29 1998

'The fans' chants of "you're not fit to wear our shirts!" could be heard in the dressing room – I hope the players were hurt by it,' was Manchester City manager Frank Clark's brutal rejoinder after his team City lost 1–0 to bottom-of-the-table Huddersfield on 8 November. A demoralised Man City gave Huddersfield little trouble as the Yorkshire side coasted to only their second of the season, with Rob Edwards tapping in a goal 14 minutes from the end. The result was sweet revenge for The Terriers, coming on the 10th anniversary of their 10–1 demolition by City in the old Second Division.

HUDDERSFIELD DAILY EXAMINER

Getting their own back: Rob Edwards scored Huddersfield's late goal

15 November: Middlesbrough's class began to show as they beat Norwich 3–1 away to move into fourth position in the league. Paul Merson was the architect of another fine Boro victory, his position in the first team only assured after Bryan Robson had quiet words with his old International teammate Glenn Hoddle and had Merson removed from the England international squad to play Cameroon. 'It doesn't mean I don't have an England future,' explained Merson, 'At least I hope not. Glenn just told me to keep playing well and keep scoring.' Merson did just that with his sixth goal in seven games.

Middlesbrough's chances of promotion get better: Craig Hignett and Neil Adams, 5/11/97

Monday November 30 1998

Tuesday December 1 1998

Wednesday December 2 1998

Thursday December 3 1998

Friday December 4 1998

Saturday December 5 1998   FA Cup round 2
Norwich City at Swindon Town

Sunday December 6 1998

Monday December 7 1998

Tuesday December 8 1998

Wednesday December 9 1998

Thursday December 10 1998

Friday December 11 1998

Saturday December 12 1998
Norwich City at Wolverhampton Wanderers

Sunday December 13 1998

Hard times in Oxford. With financial disaster looming and every player at the club placed on the transfer list it was no surprise to see them lose 2–1 at Norwich on 22 November. The nail in the coffin was supplied by The Canaries' Wales Under-21 star, teenager Craig Bellamy. But despite this dropping them into the relegation zone, Oxford put up a spirited performance and their battling captain, Mike Ford, was even able to put a positive spin on the players' uncertain futures. 'So what if we're all up for sale?' he told his players. 'If you fancy a move to a bigger club, now's your chance.'

Kevin Kilbane's £1.25m fee couldn't help the Baggies to promotion

Paul Merson's not the only player in the Nationwide League who's been rejuvenated by a drop down from the Premiership. Since his £2.5 million move from Newcastle, Lee Clark had won more man-of-the-match awards than he could remember. He'd won so many bottles of champagne that his wife had to go out and buy a drinks cabinet to keep them all in. 30 November was no exception to Clark's dazzling form as his 12th- and 14th-minute goals helped Sunderland sink struggling Tranmere 3–0 at the Stadium of Light. 'Goalscoring is 90 per cent confidence and when it is high you just watch them go in – that's what I'm doing now,' explained a delighted Clark.

Nicky Summerbee pressures Lennie Johnrose – not as much pressure as a Wembley play-off though...

Still only November and Reading's promotion challenge seemed to have already fallen away, with The Royals stuck firmly in the bottom half of the table. But football's not just about the league, and a stunning 3–2 away victory over Premiership title contenders Leeds in the Coca-Cola Cup gave Reading a quarter-final place. Despite doubts about the future of the cup, and with rumours of Coca-Cola withdrawing their sponsorship, Reading did well to earn their progression against a full-strength Leeds side. And a fortunate draw put them up against another survivor from the First Division, Middlesbrough.

'The improvement in this team has come from the confidence the players have found in themselves. We are getting it right and now we are catching up with the others,' reckoned veteran midfielder Barry Horne. The former Wales skipper had every right to be pleased with his new team, Huddersfield, as they beat Bury 2–0 at home on 30 November. The victory finally hauled a much-improved Town side off the bottom of the First Division. Paul Dalton scored both goals for Huddersfield, the first a free header and the second a simple tap-in after a goalmouth melee.

As shocks go, Reading dumping Leeds out of the Coca-Cola was a stunner

ACTION IMAGES

Confidence leads to Huddersfield improvement, reckons Barry Horne

QUIZ 3 ABOUT NORWICH CITY

1 In which season did Norwich find themselves top of the First Division after four games?
- a) 1986-87
- b) 1988-90 ✓
- c) 1990-91

2 What happened to the club car park during the Second World War?
- a) It became a temporary prisoner-of-war camp
- b) It was bombed, the Germans narrowly missing the stadium
- c) It was the site of two anti-aircraft batteries ✗ C

3 In which season did Norwich achieve their best-ever League finish of third in the Premiership?
- a) 1992-93 ✗ C
- b) 1993-94
- c) 1994-95

4 What was the name of Norwich City's first ground?
- a) The Nest
- b) The Bird Cage ✓
- c) Carrow Lane

5 Against which club did Norwich play their first League game in August 1920?
- a) Birmingham City
- b) Blackburn Rovers ✗ C
- c) Plymouth Argyle

6 Which famous TV chef is on the Carrow Road board?
- a) Ainsley Harriet
- b) Delia Smith ✓
- c) Keith Floyd

7 Which top fashion designer was behind the 1987-88 Norwich kit?
- a) Jean Paul Gaultier
- b) Bruce Oldfield ✓
- c) Laura Ashley

8 In what position did Norwich City finish their 1995-96 Division One season?
- a) 16th
- b) 18th ✗ A
- c) 20th

9 What was unusual about Norwich's position at the top of the table after 24 games of the 1992-93 Premiership season?
- a) They had five games in hand
- b) They had a negative goal difference ✗ B
- c) They had used only eleven players

10 Who played the back pass that Bryan Gunn famously missed during the 1995-96 East Anglian derby match at Ipswich season?
- a) Robert Ullathorne ✓
- b) Darren Eadie
- c) Robert Fleck

HUDDERSFIELD DAILY EXAMINER

Answers: 1.b 2.c 3.c 4.a 5.c 6.b 7.b 8.a 9.b 10.a

Monday December 14 1998

Tuesday December 15 1998

Wednesday December 16 1998

Thursday December 17 1998

Friday December 18 1998

Saturday December 19 1998
Bristol City at Norwich City

Sunday December 20 1998

Monday December 21 1998

Tuesday December 22 1998

Wednesday December 23 1998

Thursday December 24 1998

Friday December 25 1998

Saturday December 26 1998
Norwich City at Queens Park Rangers

Sunday December 27 1998

The strain was beginning to show at Portsmouth. An inauspicious run of form coincided with boardroom rumbles. Terry Venables had just seen his Australian side knocked out of the World Cup by Iran and seemed to be daggers drawn with the Pompey Board. So it was a gloomy collection of 7,500 fans who turned out to see Pompey take on Stoke at Fratton Park, and El Tel was noticeably absent. It says a lot for Portsmouth's character that they came out of the match 2–0 winners with goals from Aloisi and new signing Svensson. At least the disaffected fans had something to cheer this December.

ALLSPORT

Noticeably absent – Terry Venables still smarting over Iran

The Valley was becoming an increasingly intimidating place to visit as Christmas drew near, with barely a seat left empty in Charlton Athletic's 16,000-seater stadium for any match. Part of the credit must go to Charlton's best run of form for many a season and it was beginning to look like the team that had been so often the bridesmaid might make this the season to finally return to the top division after a 26-year absence. Certainly their 2–1 victory over promotion rivals Sheffield United on 10 December didn't hurt their chances with 'Super Clive' Mendonca adding two more goals to his impressive tally.

A rare sight in 1997-98, so Man City fans
would say, a blue shirt battles for the ball

Monday December 28 1998
Watford at Norwich City

Tuesday December 29 1998

Wednesday December 30 1998

Thursday December 31 1998

Friday January 1 1999

Saturday January 2 1999
FA Cup round 3

Sunday January 3 1999

Monday January 4 1999

Tuesday January 5 1999

Wednesday January 6 1999

Thursday January 7 1999

Friday January 8 1999

Saturday January 9 1999
Norwich City at Crewe Alexandra

Sunday January 10 1999

Oxford United's £10 million debt was still causing them nightmares off the pitch, but on it they had one solid gold asset in the form of young midfielder Joey Beauchamp. On a cold Friday night on 12 December man-of-the-match Beauchamp single-handedly destroyed Queens Park Rangers at the Manor Ground as he made one and scored two in a 3–1 victory. The pinnacle of his performance was his second goal, scored just after half-time, a beautifully lofted chip that sailed over QPR's bemused keeper, Tony Roberts, and into the back of the net.

ALLSPORT

Niall Quinn is shdowed by QPR's Steve Yates of Sunderland, 6/12/97

 Poor old Frank Clark finally had something to cheer about as Manchester City turned in an excellent performance to beat Middlesbrough at home 2–0 on 20 December. The goals were provided by Rosler and Dickov. The 27,000 loyal fans at Maine Road were delighted as Manchester City turned in their best performance of the season to outplay Middlesbrough in every part of the field. Particularly heartening for City fans was the excellent form of talismanic Kinkladze, especially as he had turned down two offers from Premiership clubs in the week and pledged to stay with City as they fought relegation.

'Georgie!' – a thorn in many sides, a heartbreaking loss for Man City fans in 1998

Monday January 11 1999

Tuesday January 12 1999

Wednesday January 13 1999

Thursday January 14 1999

Friday January 15 1999

Saturday January 16 1999
West Bromwich Albion at Norwich City

Sunday January 17 1999

Monday January 18 1999

Tuesday January 19 1999

Wednesday January 20 1999

Thursday January 21 1999

Friday January 22 1999

Saturday January 23 1999
FA Cup round 4

Sunday January 24 1999

---

20 December: Ipswich Town pulled themselves a little further out of relegation trouble with a magnificent 3–1 away victory at Port Vale. The Blues' hero was striker Alex Mathie who benefited from England Under-21 striker James Sowcroft's three-match suspension and earned his first start for a month. Mathie celebrated his 29th birthday with two goals in 12 minutes of the first half. Town manager George Burley said afterwards: 'Alex has done well and he's got at least another two games to give me even more to think about.' The game was effectively finished in the 43rd minute when Mathie's strike partner, David Johnson, made it three for Ipswich.

ALLSPORT

Wolves – one of few sides to score over a rampant Forest in 1997-98

Sheffield United proved that anything Charlton Athletic could do a fortnight ago, they could do better, with a stunning 4–1 victory at Bramall Lane over the Londoners on 28 December. Greek International full-back Vas Borbokis was the Blades' best player and had a hand in all four goals, with Gareth Taylor, Dean Saunders, Brian Deane and Nicky Marker all profiting from his skills. He was taken off after 77 minutes to a standing ovation, having run himself into the ground. Unfortunately for both sides the result left Middlesbrough and Nottingham Forest five points clear at the top as the new year began.

John Spencer's odyssey continued with a brief stay at Loftus Road, and a win over Bradford

Monday January 25 1999

Tuesday January 26 1999

Wednesday January 27 1999

Thursday January 28 1999

Friday January 29 1999

Saturday January 30 1999
Norwich City at Bolton Wanderers

Sunday January 31 1999

Monday February 1 1999

Tuesday February 2 1999

Wednesday February 3 1999

Thursday February 4 1999

Friday February 5 1999

Saturday February 6 1999
Stockport County at Norwich City

Sunday February 7 1999

There was a distinct feeling of déjà vû at the Riverside as key Brazilian midfielder Emerson went AWOL for the second year running. 'Last season it was because he had family problems. This time we are unaware of any problems,' said a tight-lipped Bryan Robson. The problems with the Brazilian star were not affecting the rest of Middlesbrough's players though, as a convincing 3–1 home win over Stockport County showed. Mikkel Beck scored two goals and Hignett one as Boro romped home. They ended the year league leaders on goal difference despite Forest's Pierre Van Hooijdonk's 20 goals thus far.

Another absence from Emerson didn't spoil Boro's party

ALLSPORT

'Some of the players will have to go – decisions need to be made and they will be. A good team would have gone on and won after taking the lead. But we're not a good team.' That was the verdict of a close-to-tears Steve McMahon after lowly GM Vauxhall Conference Stevenage Borough knocked Swindon out of the FA Cup at the County Ground, on 3 January 1998. Jason Solomon and Guiliano Grazioli were the Stevenage goalscorers who ended Swindon's run at the first hurdle as they crashed to a 2–1 defeat in appalling weather. But the swirling wind and driving rain were no excuse and Swindon deserved to lose.

Celebration time for lowly Stevenage after taking Swindon out. Newcastle soon...

ALLSPORT

'Reggae Boy': Paul Hall helps Pompey to a share of the 2–2 spoils against an apathetic Villa

'I was in a no-win situation. I really wanted to win the game but there are important fixtures coming up for us,' said Forest boss Dave Bassett as he explained why Steve Stone, Ian Woan and Andy Johnson were left out of the Forest side who lost 4–1 to Charlton in the third round of the FA Cup on 3 January. Charlton demolished a scrappy Forest side with goals for John Robinson, Steve Brown, Clive Mendonca and Carl Leaburn. Pierre Van Hooijdonk came on as a second-half substitute for Forest and scored his 21st of the season, but Forest never looked like troubling the Addicks.

Paul Furlong's devastating hat-trick in the second half put the seal on the most comprehensive victory of the season. Struggling Stoke – two months without a win – were at home to in-form Birmingham City on 10 January. Stoke soon had their backs to the wall as Blues midfielder Bryan Hughes opened their account with two superbly-taken goals early in the first half. Nicky Forster added another before the whistle and in the second half Furlong scored his hat-trick and Jon McCarthy added one more to make the scoreline 0–7. 'Seven goals is a thrashing by anyone's standards. You just can't believe it,' said downcast Stoke Boss Chic Bates.

Clive Walker celebrates yet another of his many Cup 'stories' as the non-leaguers hold Reading 1–1

QUIZ 4 ABOUT DIVISION ONE

1 What record number of players did Birmingham City use in their 1995-96 Division One campaign?
- a) 29
- b) 32
- a) 46

2 Who were Division One Champions in 1993?
- a) Ipswich Town
- b) Crystal Palace
- c) Barnsley

3 In what season did big-spending Middlesbrough first win promotion to the Premiership?
- a) 1994
- b) 1995
- c) 1996

4 By what score did Crystal Palace beat Sheffield United in the 1997 Play-off Final?
- a) 1–0
- b) 2–0
- c) 3–0

5 In what year did the top clubs break away from the Football League?
- a) 1990
- b) 1991
- c) 1992

6 Who were Division One champions that year?
- a) Newcastle United
- b) Blackburn Rovers
- c) Swindon Town

7 How many clubs are there in Division One today?
- a) 20
- b) 22
- c) 24

8 Which club scored 100 goals in their 1996-97 Division One Campaign?
- a) Bolton Wanderers
- b) Barnsley
- c) Crystal Palace

9 Who topped the Division One goalscoring charts for the 1996-97 season?
- a) Steve Bull
- b) Trevor Morely
- c) John McGinlay

10 Who finished bottom of the table that season?
- a) Grimsby Town
- b) Oldham Athletic
- c) Southend United

ALLSPORT

Answers: 1.a 2.b 3.b 4.a 5.c 6.a 7.c 8.a 9.c 10.c

Monday February 8 1999

Tuesday February 9 1999

Wednesday February 10 1999

Thursday February 11 1999

Friday February 12 1999

Saturday February 13 1999
Barnsley at Norwich City   FA Cup round 5

Sunday February 14 1999

Monday February 15 1999

Tuesday February 16 1999

Wednesday February 17 1999

Thursday February 18 1999

Friday February 19 1999

Saturday February 20 1999
Norwich City at Bury

Sunday February 21 1999

Sunderland finally started to show some of their Premiership quality and began a long haul towards the promotion places with a fine home performance to beat Sheffield United 4–2 on 10 January. Niall Quinn was in particularly impressive form, supporting boss Peter Reid's view that if he had been fit at the end of the previous season Sunderland would not have been relegated. But it wasn't just the old warhorse who was having a good day. Young Kevin Phillips scored two and Lee Clark remained in the impressive form he'd shown ever since moving to Sunderland.

ACTION IMAGES

Crewe put two past Swindon Town in this home game

Bury were having real difficulty in finding the net with the worst goalscoring record in the division. And at home to Stockport on 18 January, it was left to County front-man Brett Angell to show them how to do it. His beautiful volley from a Paul Cook cross lit up an otherwise dreary afternoon and provided the only goal of the game. Bury had good reason to believe themselves jinxed though as they hit woodwork twice in the last five minutes but still failed to score. Only their decent defensive record was keeping them out of serious relegation trouble.

'Abou! Abou!' – a Hammers' favourite even before the FA Cup game versus Man City

ALLSPORT

Monday February 22 1999

Tuesday February 23 1999

Wednesday February 24 1999

Thursday February 25 1999

Friday February 26 1999

Saturday February 27 1999
Sheffield United at Norwich City

Sunday February 28 1999

Monday March 1 1999

Tuesday March 2 1999
Norwich City at Birmingham City

Wednesday March 3 1999

Thursday March 4 1999

Friday March 5 1999

Saturday March 6 1999
Norwich City at Sunderland   FA Cup quarter-finals

Sunday March 7 1999

Port Vale had nearly succeeded in giving Arsenal a real scare in the FA Cup in mid-week and the resulting morale boost turned them into a too-hot-to-handle team for a home match against fellow strugglers Portsmouth. Pompey were still reeling from the double shock of losing chairman Terry Venables and manager Terry Fenwick and came out 2–1 losers to goals from Stewart Talbot and Lee Mills. 'It was tense out there,' admitted Vale manager John Rudge who was obviously relieved that his side had ended their run of seven consecutive league defeats.

A clean sheet against Arsenal for keeper Paul Musselwhite

Ipswich's 5–0 thrashing of Norwich on 21 January equalled their biggest ever derby win, something they've now achieved three times. It was also their second five-goal victory in as many home games. A superb hat-trick before half-time from Alex Mathie was the icing on a very fruity cake, with Dutch Winger Bobby Petta providing the other two goals in a demoliton of the Canaries' defence. A delighted George Burley sounded a warning to other teams in the division: 'We have got so many talented young players here that I think we have got a great future at the club. These are exciting times for Ipswich.'

Jamie Moreno scores Middlesbrough's second goal in a 2–1 defeat of Stoke City, 1/2/98

Monday March 8 1999

Tuesday March 9 1999
Port Vale at Norwich City

Wednesday March 10 1999

Thursday March 11 1999

Friday March 12 1999

Saturday March 13 1999
Norwich City at Bradford City

Sunday March 14 1999

Monday March 15 1999

Tuesday March 16 1999

Wednesday March 17 1999

Thursday March 18 1999

Friday March 19 1999

Saturday March 20 1999
Portsmouth at Norwich City

Sunday March 21 1999

A standing ovation greeted Alan Ball's return to Fratton Park as Portsmouth hoped to put Terry Venables' losing legacy behind them. Rooted to the bottom of the division, Pompey struggled to a 1–1 draw against Sheffield United, despite the Blades having keeper Simon Tracey sent off just before half-time. Despite the disappointing result, Pompey's goalscoring Aussie, Craig Foster, was full of praise for Ball, and said 'The first thing he has done is to restore confidence and self-belief among the players.' Unfortunately the match is more likely to be remembered for the attack on an assistant referee by a Blades fan after Tracey's dismissal.

ACTION IMAGES

Is that James Scowcroft in David Holdsworth's eye?

Chris Kamara's unhappy departure as Bradford's manager could have knocked the wind out of the Bantams' promotion challenge. But new boss Paul Jewell proved he had an eye for quality players by offering Robbie Blake a lucrative three-year contract with the club. Blake responded with four goals in eight games, including the one that threw a spanner in the works of visiting side Charlton's promotion hopes on 7 February. A 1–0 victory moved Bradford to within striking distance of the play-off places and took hapless Charlton down a peg or two in their third game running without a goal.

Division One FA Cup clashes are often battles of will rather than skill and this was a replay!

Monday March 22 1999

Tuesday March 23 1999

Wednesday March 24 1999

Thursday March 25 1999

Friday March 26 1999

Saturday March 27 1999
Norwich City at Huddersfield Town

Sunday March 28 1999

Monday March 29 1999

Tuesday March 30 1999

Wednesday March 31 1999

Thursday April 1 1999

Friday April 2 1999

Saturday April 3 1999
Crystal Palace at Norwich City

Sunday April 4 1999

A hard-earned point at home against Middlesbrough on 7 February was seen by many as the turning point for Birmingham City. In 20 months in charge, Trevor Francis had dumped 28 of the players he inherited and spent £12 million to try and turn the Midlands club around. He finally appeared to be getting some reward for his efforts as a feisty Birmingham side fought league leaders Middlesbrough bravely. None was braver than John McCarthy who collided with Boro's keeper, Mark Schwarzer, while scoring the opening goal. Nottingham Forest capitalised on the draw to go on top again.

FA Cup 5th round: Sheffield United 1–0 Reading, 13/2/98

They say there's a gypsy curse that's haunted Maine Road ever since Romanies were evicted to make way for its building in 1923. You could believe it too as, on 14 February, Manchester City were into the relegation zone by a headed goal from Bury's defender Paul Butler, himself a lifelong Man City fan. 'I'm City through and through and have been since I was five,' said Butler, who although unhappy to have contributed to his favourite team's current troubles, was more than delighted to have handed Bury a much-needed first win in 17 games.

Nottingham Forest's 3–0 defeat of Huddersfield puts them nearer the top: Jenkins and Rogers

Bobby Ford gets away from Dele Adebola; but Birmingham win

ALLSPORT

22 February: It was as rare as a World Cup Ticket – Michael Johnson scored his first senior goal in 250 appearances to help Birmingham put paid to Sheffield United's impressive eight-game unbeaten record. He hammered the ball into the roof of the net after being left unmarked in the six-yard area. Martin Grainger scored the other as the Blues beat the Blades 2–0 at St Andrews. 'It was a powerful performance and we never allowed Sheffield any control,' maintained Trevor Francis. The win moved Birmingham into 8th place in the league, within striking distance of the play-offs.

Port Vale's away form looked up after this 1–0 defeat of QPR

ACTION IMAGES

24 February: Ipswich's surge of form continued apace with their second five-goal home victory in four days. The recipients of the punishment were Oxford this time, and with Alex Mathie restricting himself to a single goal, it was David Johnson's turn to score a hat-trick – the first of his professional career. It wasn't all one-way traffic this time though, Oxford managed to score two goals themselves and took an early lead from the head of striker Kevin Francis past stand-in goalie Matt Holland. Midfielder Holland had to step in after a sixth minute injury to Ipswich's England Under-21 regular Richard Wright.

QUIZ 5 REFEREE QUIZ

1 According to FIFA, what is the minimum length of a pitch used in an international game?
 a) 90 metres
 b) 95 metres
 c) 100 metres

2 What is the acceptable pressure of a football?
 a) 0.6 to 1.1 atmospheres
 b) 0.5 to 1.25 atmospheres
 c) 0.75 to 2 atmospheres

3 Is the red attacking number 10 offside in this Diagram?

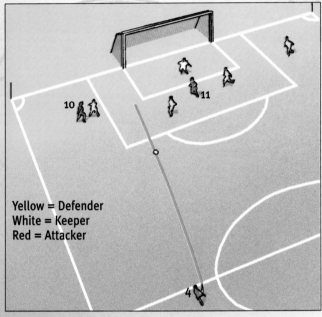

Yellow = Defender
White = Keeper
Red = Attacker

 a) No
 b) Yes
 c) Yes, but he's not interfering with play

4 When needs to go to penalties, who decides which end they are to be taken from?
 a) A toss of a coin before the game begins
 b) The referee decides
 c) A toss of a coin before the penalties are taken

5 If, during a penalty shoot-out, the keeper is injured and all substitutes have been used already, who replaces the keeper?
 a) A substitute keeper
 b) No one
 c) One of the outfield players

6 Your free-kick specialist takes a corner by flicking the ball in the air and curling it into the goal. What does the referee do?
 a) Awards the goal as fair
 b) Awards an indirect free-kick to the opposition (the corner taker is only allowed to touch the ball once until another player touches it).
 c) Awards a direct free-kick to the opposition (the corner taker is only allowed to touch the ball once until another player touches it).

7 Your keeper takes a free-kick but trips and the ball doesn't make it out of the area. What should the ref do?
 a) Has it taken again
 b) Allows play to continue
 c) Awards an indirect free-kick to the opposition

8 An opposition player persistently stands nose-to-nose with one of your team who is trying to take a throw-in, what should the referee do?
 a) Get the opposition player to stand 10-yards back
 b) Award an indirect free-kick to your team
 c) Caution the opposition player and give him a yellow card

9 What is the referee awarding in this Diagram?
 a) An indirect free-kick
 b) A corner
 c) A direct free-kick

10 If an indirect free-kick goes straight into the goal, what should the referee do?
 a) Have the kick re-taken
 b) Award an indirect free-kick to the opposition
 c) Award a goal kick

Answers: 1.c 2.a 3.a 4.b 5.c 6.b 7.a 8.c 9.a 10.c

Monday April 5 1999
Norwich City at Grimsby Town

Tuesday April 6 1999

Wednesday April 7 1999

Thursday April 8 1999

Friday April 9 1999

Saturday April 10 1999   Sunday April 11 1999
Ipswich Town at Norwich City   FA Cup semi-finals

Monday April 12 1999

Tuesday April 13 1999

Wednesday April 14 1999

Thursday April 15 1999

Friday April 16 1999

Saturday April 17 1999   Sunday April 18 1999
Tranmere Rovers at Norwich City

To call Leeds United 'giants' might be pushing the point nearly as much as calling Wolves 'giant killers,' yet the feeling at Elland Road was that there was no way for the home team to lose this FA Cup clash. Neither team caught hold of the game in the first half – Leeds obviously missed the imagination of Aussie international Harry Kewell, while Wolves seemed happy just to maintain a clean sheet. The second was similar until the dying minutes when Don Goodman's strike silenced the Leeds Kop momentarily. The Yorkshire crowd was finally sent into the Black Country depths when controversial keeper Hans Segers managed to stop a weak Hasselbaink penalty kick, and Wolves carried Division One hopes through to a semi-final appearance at Villa Park against Arsenal.

ALLSPORT

Shaun Newton, Premiership-bound although he doesn't know it here

'Of course I'm pleased but talk is cheap. There's a lot of work to do yet,' was Dave Bassett's typically taciturn response to Nottingham Forest's best display of the season so far. With Steve Stone finally back in the side again, Forest demolished fellow championship hopefuls Middlesbrough 4–0 at the City Ground on 8 March. Pierre Van Hooijdonk confirmed his reputation as the most prolific goalscorer in English football with two more to take his tally to 28 for the season. Kevin Campbell and Colin Cooper were the other two Forest players to get on the scoresheet in a 31 minute period of the second half where Forest were rampant.

'Talk is cheap' maybe, but action speaks volumes – Boro tonk Forest 4–0

Monday April 19 1999

Tuesday April 20 1999

Wednesday April 21 1999

Thursday April 22 1999

Friday April 23 1999

Saturday April 24 1999
Norwich City at Oxford United

Sunday April 25 1999

Monday April 26 1999

Tuesday April 27 1999

Wednesday April 28 1999

Thursday April 29 1999

Friday April 30 1999

Saturday May 1 1999
Swindon Town at Norwich City

Sunday May 2 1999

Poor Reading looked destined for the Second Division after Sheffield United beat them 4–0 at Bramall Lane on 15 March, despite The Blades looking far from their best. Even United's new manager Steve Thompson was forced to admit: 'If we'd played anyone decent we'd have lost.' Wayne Quinn scored the best goal of the game in the dying seconds following strikes from Graham Stuart, Marcelo and Gareth Taylor. The win put United into the play-off position with two matches in hand on all their rivals and left Reading struggling second from bottom.

Hooijdonk – didn't just strike fear into Birmingham City last season

The FA Cup quarter-final – Sheffield United versus Coventry City, 17 March. It was, of course, St Patrick's Day. So nobody should have been particularly surprised that Sheffield United's Irish goalkeeper Alan Kelly should have enjoyed some of the luck for which his countrymen are famous and saved three penalties from Dion Dublin, David Burrows and Simon Hayworth in the shootout that decided the fixture. The match was already a replay, and was sent into extra time only by skipper David Holdsworth's 89th minute goal. But it was Kelly's heroics that made sure of the Blades' place in the semis.

The Blades were sharp in battle, but penalties decided this encounter in their favour

Monday May 3 1999

Tuesday May 4 1999

Wednesday May 5 1999

Thursday May 6 1999

Friday May 7 1999

Saturday May 8 1999

Sunday May 9 1999
Norwich City at Bristol City

Monday May 10 1999

Tuesday May 11 1999

Wednesday May 12 1999

Thursday May 13 1999

Friday May 14 1999

Saturday May 15 1999

Sunday May 16 1999

21 March: When asked what his keeper Alan Miller had been trying to do, West Brom's manager Dennis Smith could only say: 'He was throwing the ball into the net!' Poor Miller handed Port Vale the equaliser that gave them a vital point in their battle against relegation in the final minute of their encounter at The Hawthorns. West Brom had been ahead twice with goals from Flynn and Taylor, but both times they let Port Vale back into the game. Jansson was the first to profit and after Miller lost the ball from a cross it was Foyle who tapped home the last-minute equaliser.

ALLSPORT

Norwich's Daryl Sutch tangos with Middlesbrough's Alun Armstrong

Hans Seger may have been the penalty-saving hero of Wolves' FA Cup competition, but the veteran keeper proved himself fallible against Arsenal in the FA Cup semi-final on 5 April. He had to take some responsibility for the Chris Wreh goal that settled this match; looking for a quick counter-attack he launched a goal-kick that fell to the feet of Patrick Vieira. Vieira drew Curle and Richards before passing to Wreh, who scored. Wolves had some chances, Goodman looked to be clear in the area after Seaman dropped a cross and Bull came on and created havoc in the penalty area, but neither chance was taken.

Sedgley versus Winterburn – an ancient battle from North London days is rejoined

Monday May 17 1999

Tuesday May 18 1999

Wednesday May 19 1999

Thursday May 20 1999

Friday May 21 1999

Saturday May 22 1999
FA Cup Final

Sunday May 23 1999

Monday May 24 1999

Tuesday May 25 1999

Wednesday May 26 1999

Thursday May 27 1999

Friday May 28 1999

Saturday May 29 1999

Sunday May 30 1999

A brave attempt by the Blades to put Newcastle out of the FA Cup ended in 1–0 defeat on 5 April, with the inevitable Alan Shearer goal being the difference between the two sides. Shearer scored in the 60th minute after a dominating passage of play, but the goal seemed to wake Sheffield United up and the last few minutes of the game must have seemed to last an eternity for the toon army as Graham Stuart and Wayne Quinn laid siege to the Newcastle goal. Only spirited defending by Newcastle's outstanding Greek defender Nikos Dabizas and superb goalkeeping by Shay Given denied the Blades extra time.

Speed over Borbokis: Newcastle stayed in the FA Cup

Paul Gascoigne had certainly made an impact at Middlesbrough. Two bookings in his first two games and then, with the end of the season looming and Middlesbrough desperate for points he had to come off in his third match with a bruised foot. Worse still, Sheffield United contrived to take all three points from them at Bramall Lane when veteran striker Dean Saunders fired in a punched-clear free kick from two yards out. Sheffield United moved firmly into play-off contention and left Boro looking at the same prospect, when they had previously hoped for the second automatic promotion place behind Forest.

Is that another yellow card coming up? Paul Gascoigne making his mark for Middlesbrough

ACTION IMAGES

Don Goodman takes on Phil Parkinson in usual committed style: Wolves 3 – Reading 1

Boro's promotion rivals Nottingham Forest reinforced their Premiership credentials as they raced six points clear of the chasing pack. A 0–3 win against Bradford City at The Pulse Stadium on 12 April was sealed by goals from Kevin Campbell, Scott Gemmill and Chris Bart-Williams. Forest manager Dave Bassett remained his usual circumspect self saying: 'We can see the winning post, but horses at the front can fall and experience has taught me to take nothing for granted.' More good news for Forest was that Colin Cooper's suspected cruciate ligament injury sustained in this match turned out to be less serious than had been feared.

'We came good today,' was Norwich City manager Mike Walker's verdict as the Canaries guaranteed their third season in the First Division with a thundering 5–0 win over Huddersfield Town at Carrow Road on 13 April. Iwan Roberts scored twice against his old club, and Craig Fleming, Neil Adams and Erik Fuglestad chipped in with the other three. Fleming's goal was the first of the afternoon – he scored after 13 minutes with a header with the second league goal of his professional career. There was more injury trouble for Norwich's Darren Eadie who had to leave the field with a suspected fractured cheekbone.

'Mers' – Paul Merson's new attitude to life took him from Boro to France 98

Quiz 6 About Division One

1 Which company sponsored the Football League before Nationwide?
- a) Endsleigh
- b) Carling
- c) Littlewoods ✓

2 Which club gained promotion to the Premiership in 1994 and again in 1996?
- a) Bolton Wanderers
- b) Sunderland
- c) Leicester City ✗ C

3 Ludek Miklosko won promotion with which two clubs?
- a) West Ham United and Derby County
- b) Leicester City and Sunderland
- c) Leicester City and Oxford United ✗ C

4 Who was manager of Nottingham Forest when they were relegated to Division One in 1993?
- a) Frank Clark
- b) Brian Clough ✗ B
- c) Dave Bassett

5 Who were Division One Champions in 1996?
- a) Nottingham Forest
- b) Sheffield United ✗ C
- c) Sunderland

6 Who was Nottingham Forest's top scorer in their 1993-1994 promotion season?
- a) Stan Collymore ✓
- b) Andrea Silenzi
- c) Pierre Van Hooijdonk

7 Joachim and Walsh played in a Play-off Final for which team?
- a) Charlton Athletic
- b) Ipswich Town ✓
- c) Leicester City

8 Goals by Deane and Agana took which club into the top flight?
- a) Sheffield United ✓
- b) Sunderland
- c) Birmingham City

9 Who has the largest average home gates in Division One?
- a) Birmingham City
- b) Bristol City
- c) Wolverhampton Wanderers ✗ C

10 In what season were Birmingham City promoted to Division One?
- a) 1994
- b) 1995 ✓
- c) 1996

ALLSPORT

Monday May 31 1999

Tuesday June 1 1999

Wednesday June 2 1999

Thursday June 3 1999

Friday June 4 1999

Saturday June 5 1999

Sunday June 6 1999

Monday June 7 1999

Tuesday June 8 1999

Wednesday June 9 1999

Thursday June 10 1999

Friday June 11 1999

Saturday June 12 1999

Sunday June 13 1999

Charlton continued their charge towards a potential automatic promotion place with a scrappy 1–0 win over Portsmouth at The Valley. This seventh victory in a row was won by a Steve Jones header at the far post just after half-time, but neither side really gained the upper hand in the match and the result could have been different if Portsmouth's young Jamaican, Paul Hall, had taken his gilt-covered opportunity to equalise seconds before the final whistle. After the match Portsmouth manager Alan Ball was moved to describe Charlton as: 'An object lesson for everyone. It's phenomenal what they've done.'

A Steve Jones header gave Charlton a 1–0 lead over Portsmouth

Nottingham Forest won the First Division championship in an edgy 1–0 victory over Reading at The City ground on 26 April. In the process they knocked Reading down into Division Two. An off-colour Forest side struggled to get a grip of the game, and it was left to Chris Bart-Williams to provide a moment of great skill with a beautiful turn and volley to settle the game in the 87th minute. The pitch invasion afterwards was inspired more by relief than euphoria. For manager Dave Bassett this was a record-setting seventh promotion for a side he'd been in charge of.

Lee Clarke of Sunderland and Mick Stockwell of Ipswich – still fighting for promotion

Monday June 14 1999

Tuesday June 15 1999

Wednesday June 16 1999

Thursday June 17 1999

Friday June 18 1999

Saturday June 19 1999   Sunday June 20 1999

Monday June 21 1999

Tuesday June 22 1999

Wednesday June 23 1999

Thursday June 24 1999

Friday June 25 1999

Saturday June 26 1999   Sunday June 27 1999

While Dutch striker Pierre Van Hooijdonk at Nottingham Forest had stolen the limelight with his 34 goals this season, there was another player scoring extremely well. Young Kevin Phillips of Sunderland made it 31 so far by scoring two goals in the 3–0 victory over Stoke City at the Stadium of Light. In front of a record crowd of 41,214 he and Darren Williams secured three points and left Sunderland firmly in the promotion chase. He also displayed superb attitude when commenting after the match: 'My only target is to get this club back into the Premiership.'

*Aiming for the limelight:
Kevin Phillips gets his 31st*

'We've had the relegation and three cup final defeats in the last year so we needed a day like this' – Bryan Robson was obviously a relieved man as Middlesbrough, on 3 May, managed to capture second place in the First Division and an automatic promotion. A 4–1 defeat of Oxford United in front of a record crowd at the Riverside gave him and his players the prize they valued more than any other, a season in the top flight where they feel they belong. Two goals apiece from Alun Armstrong and Craig Hignett gave Middlesbrough the result they desperately needed.

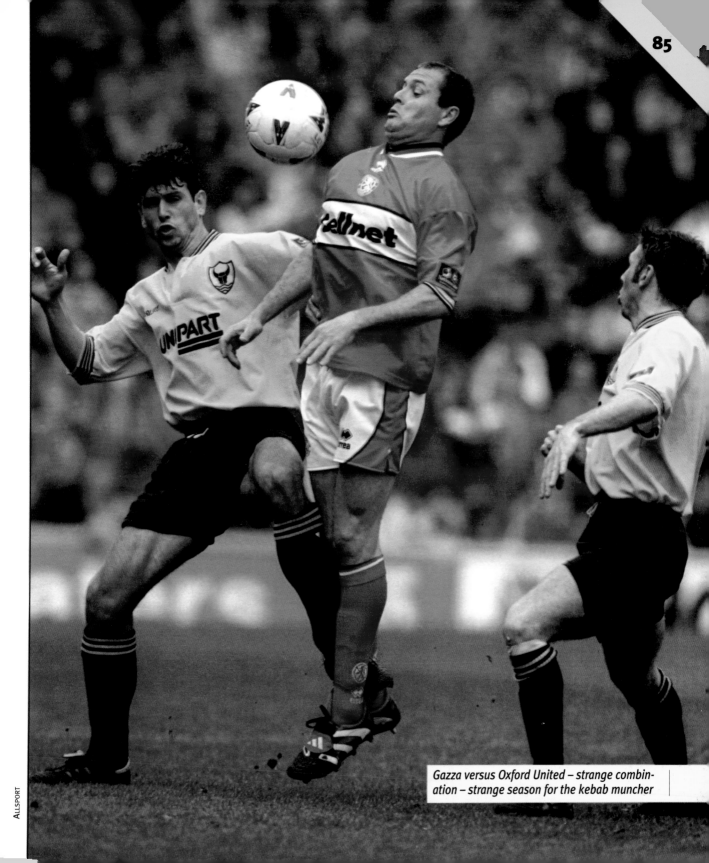

Gazza versus Oxford United – strange combination – strange season for the kebab muncher

Monday June 28 1999

Tuesday June 29 1999

Wednesday June 30 1999

Thursday July 1 1999

Friday July 2 1999

Saturday July 3 1999   Sunday July 4 1999

'We'll meet again,' sang the combined fans of Stoke and Manchester Cities as both teams were relegated at the end of a thrilling 5–2 victory for Manchester City at the Britannia Stadium on 3 May. As results from other grounds went against the doomed pair, a sense of resignation set in. 'That seems to sum up our season,' said Blues manager Joe Royle facing the club's lowest league position in their 111-year history. 'Our best performance of the season, but everything goes against us elsewhere.' Stoke caretaker boss Alan Durban was more resigned, saying: 'We'd already hit the iceberg before I came in.'

With one of the dullest FA Cup finals since the last one having been played out on the sacred turf, neutrals already felt that the only thing to look forward to now was the World Cup. Who would really be interested in a Division One play-off that Sunderland were going to walk away with? So those 'football fans' who couldn't find a TV to sit in front of or a Wembley ticket to clutch will always rue the missed 120 minutes that featured eight superb goals, the best hat-trick ever seen at Wembley, a fairy-tale story of rags to riches, tears for the media favourites and applause from both sets of fans for the winners.

This was undoubtedly one of the greatest games ever to be played in the nation's capital. It had everything from Sunderland-born Charlton striker Clive Mendonca's peerless hat-trick breaking his own family's heart, to Michael Gray's missed penalty. The action was fast but not furious, the skill levels made Newcastle's FA Cup performance look even more tired and unimaginative than hindsight suggested and the result was always too close to call. Whether Sunderland will 'do a Barnsley' this campaign is open to question, but whatever happens this season, anyone who witnessed this game has good cause to remember 1997/98 as a monument to great Division One football.

Nottingham Forest make it back to top flight football, although West Brom held them to a 1–1 draw on 3/5/98. This is Steve Stone

*Ipswich learns patience as Charlton Athletic
join the Premier League for the 1998/99 season*

		DATE	SCORE	POINTS	PLACE	REFEREE
Norwich City ..v .... Barnsley	HOME	/ /	–			
	AWAY	/ /	–			
Norwich City ..v .... Birmingham City	HOME	/ /	–			
	AWAY	/ /	–			
Norwich City ..v .... Bolton Wanderers	HOME	/ /	–			
	AWAY	/ /	–			
Norwich City ..v............. Bradford City	HOME	/ /	–			
	AWAY	/ /	–			
Norwich City ..v .... Bristol City	HOME	/ /	–			
	AWAY	/ /	–			
Norwich City ..v.................... Bury	HOME	/ /	–			
	AWAY	/ /	–			
Norwich City ..v......... Crewe Alexandra	HOME	/ /	–			
	AWAY	/ /	–			
Norwich City ..v............ Crystal Palace	HOME	/ /	–			
	AWAY	/ /	–			
Norwich City ..v............ Grimsby Town	HOME	/ /	–			
	AWAY	/ /	–			
Norwich City ..v........ Huddersfield Town	HOME	/ /	–			
	AWAY	/ /	–			
Norwich City ..v .... Ipswich Town	HOME	/ /	–			
	AWAY	/ /	–			
Norwich City ..v............ Oxford United	HOME	/ /	–			
	AWAY	/ /	–			
Norwich City ..v .... Port Vale	HOME	/ /	–			
	AWAY	/ /	–			
Norwich City ..v.............. Portsmouth	HOME	/ /	–			
	AWAY	/ /	–			
Norwich City ..v ..... Queens Park Rangers	HOME	/ /	–			
	AWAY	/ /	–			
Norwich City ..v.......... Sheffield United	HOME	/ /	–			
	AWAY	/ /	–			
Norwich City ..v......... Stockport County	HOME	/ /	–			
	AWAY	/ /	–			
Norwich City ..v.............. Sunderland	HOME	/ /	–			
	AWAY	/ /	–			
Norwich City ..v............ Swindon Town	HOME	/ /	–			
	AWAY	/ /	–			
Norwich City ..v .... Tranmere Rovers	HOME	/ /	–			
	AWAY	/ /	–			
Norwich City ..v................. Watford	HOME	/ /	–			
	AWAY	/ /	–			
Norwich City ..v..... West Bromwich Albion	HOME	/ /	–			
	AWAY	/ /	–			
Norwich City ..v. Wolverhampton Wanderers	HOME	/ /	–			
	AWAY	/ /	–			

SCORERS	RED CARDS	YELLOW CARDS	COMMENTS

SUPPORTERS' AWAY INFORMATION

UNITED KINGDOM AIRPORTS

Aberdeen (Dyce)	01224 722331
Belfast (Aldegrove)	01849 422888
Birmingham International	0121 767-5511
Blackpool	01253 343434
Bournemouth (Hurn)	01202 593939
Bristol (Luisgate)	01275 474444
Cambridge	01223 61133
Cardiff	01446 711211
East Midlands	01332 852852
Edinburgh	0131333-1000
Glasgow	0141 887 1111
Humberside	01652 688491
Inverness (Dalcross)	01463 232471
Leeds & Bradford (Yeadon)	01132 509696
Liverpool (Speke)	0151 486-8877
London (Gatwick)	01293 535353

London (Heathrow)	0181 759-4321
London (London City)	0171 474-5555
London (Stanstead)	01279 680500
Luton	01582 405100
Lydd	01797 320401
Manchester (Ringway)	0161 489-3000
Newcastle (Woolsington)	0191 286-0966
Newquay (St. Mawgan)	01637 860551
Norwich	01603 411923
Plymouth	01752 772752
Prestwick	01292 479822
Southampton	01703 629600
Southend	01702 340201
Stornoway	01851 702256
Teesside (Darlington)	01325 332811
Westland Heliport	0171 228-0181

PASSPORT OFFICES

London 0171 799-2728
Clive House, 70–78 Petty France, SW1H 9HD
Liverpool 0151 237-3010
5th Floor, India Buildings, Water Street, L2 0QZ
Peterborough 01733 555688
UK Passport Agency, Aragon Court,
Northminster Road, Peterborough PE1 1QG
Glasgow 0141 332-4441
3 Northgate, 96 Milton Street, Cowcadens,
Glasgow G4 0BT
Newport 01633 473700
Olympia House, Upper Dock Street, Newport,
Gwent NP9 1XQ
Belfast 01232 330214
Hampton House, 47–53 High Street,
Belfast BT1 2QS

TOURIST & TRAVEL INFORMATION CENTRES

ENGLAND
Birmingham (NEC)	0121 780-4321
Blackpool	01253 21623
Bournemouth	01202 789789
Brighton	01273 323755
Cambridge	01223 322640
Chester	01244 351609
Colchester	01206 282920
Dover	01304 205108
Durham	0191 384-3720
Hull	01482 223559
Lancaster	01524 32878
Leicester	01162 650555
Lincoln	01522 529828
Liverpool	0151 708-8838
Manchester	0161 234-3157
Newcastle-upon-Tyne	0191 261-0691
Newquay	01603 871345
Norwich	01603 666071
Oxford	01865 726871
Portsmouth	01705 826722
Southampton	01703 221106
Torquay	01803 297428
York	01904 620557

SCOTLAND
Aberdeen	01224 632727
Edinburgh	0131 557-1700
Glasgow	0141 848-4440
Stirling	01786 475019

WALES
Cardiff	01222 227281
Wrexham	01978 292015

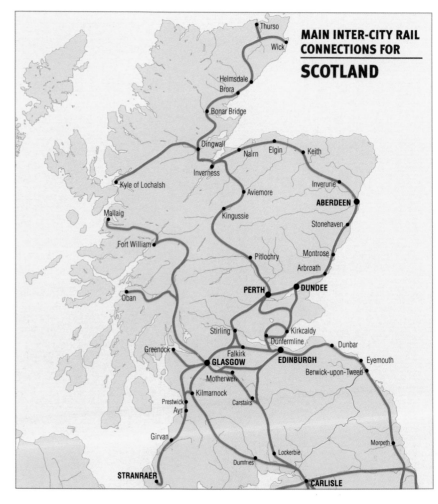

MAIN INTER-CITY RAIL CONNECTIONS FOR SCOTLAND

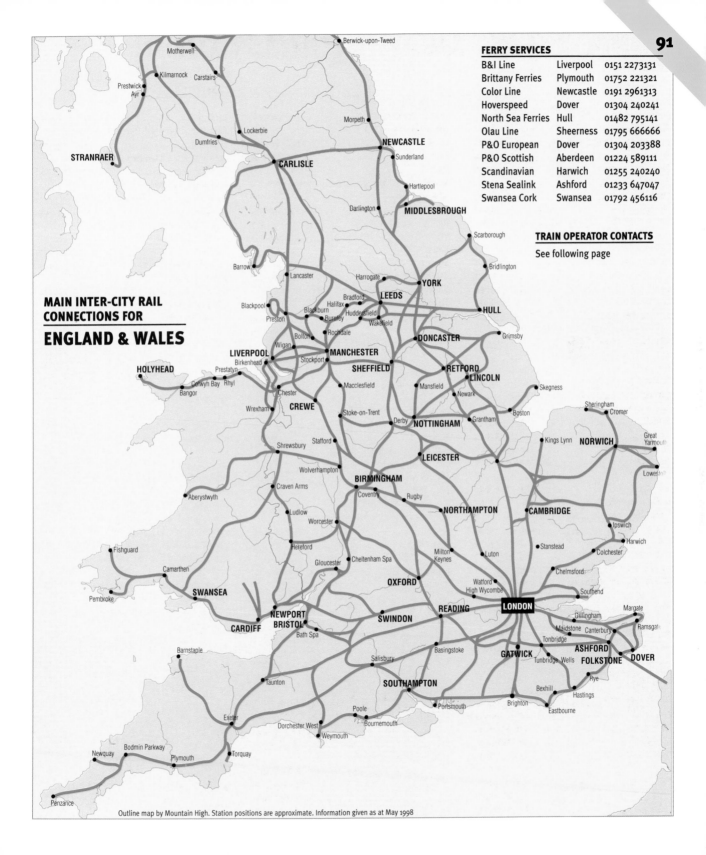

MAIN INTER-CITY RAIL CONNECTIONS FOR ENGLAND & WALES

FERRY SERVICES

B&I Line	Liverpool	0151 2273131
Brittany Ferries	Plymouth	01752 221321
Color Line	Newcastle	0191 2961313
Hoverspeed	Dover	01304 240241
North Sea Ferries	Hull	01482 795141
Olau Line	Sheerness	01795 666666
P&O European	Dover	01304 203388
P&O Scottish	Aberdeen	01224 589111
Scandinavian	Harwich	01255 240240
Stena Sealink	Ashford	01233 647047
Swansea Cork	Swansea	01792 456116

TRAIN OPERATOR CONTACTS

See following page

Outline map by Mountain High. Station positions are approximate. Information given as at May 1998

SUPPORTERS' AWAY INFORMATION

TRAIN OPERATORS

ANGLIA RAILWAYS
15-25 Artillery Lane, London, E1 7HA
Tel 01473 693333
Fax 01473 693497

CARDIFF RAILWAY CO
10th Floor, Brunel House, 2 Fitzalan Rd,
Cardiff CF2 1SA
Tel 01222 430000
Fax 01222 480463

CENTRAL TRAINS
PO Box 4323, Stanier House, 10 Holliday Street
Birmingham B1 1TH
Tel 0121 654 4444
Fax 0121 654 4461

CHILTERN RAILWAY CO
Western House, 14 Rickfords Hill, Aylesbury
HP20 2RX
Tel 01296 332100
Fax 01296 332126

CONNEX SOUTH CENTRAL
Stephenson House, 2 Cherry Orchard Road,
Croydon CR9 6JB
Tel 0181 667 2780
Fax 0181 667 2906

EUROSTAR (UK)
Eurostar House, Waterloo Station, London
SE1 8SE
Tel 0171 928 5151

GATWICK EXPRESS
52 Grosvenor Gardens, London SW1W 0AU
Tel 0171 973 5005
Fax 0171 973 5038

GREAT EASTERN RAILWAY
Hamilton House, 3 Appold Street, London
EC2A 2AA
Tel 0645 50 50 00
Fax 01473 693745

GREAT NORTH EATERN RAILWAY
Main Headquarters Building, York YO1 1HT
Tel 01904 653022
Fax 01904 523392

GREAT WESTERN TRAINS CO
Milford House, 1 Milton Street, Swindon SN1 1HL
Tel 01793 499400
Fax 01793 499460

HEATHROW EXPRESS
4th Floor, Cardinal Point, Newall Rd, Hounslow
Middlesex TW6 2QS
Tel 0181 745 0578
Fax 0181 745 1627

ISLAND LINE
Ryde St Johns Road Station, Ryde, Isle Of Wight
PO33 2BA
Tel 01983 812591
Fax 01983 817879

LTS RAIL
Central House, Clifftown Road, Southend-on-Sea
SS1 1AB
Tel 01702 357889

MERSEYRAIL ELECTRICS
Rail House, Lord Nelson Street, Liverpool L1 1JF
Tel 0151 709 8292
Fax 0151 702 2413

MIDLAND MAINLINE
Midland House, Nelson Street, Derby,
East Midlands DE1 2SA
Tel 0345 221125
Fax 01332 262011

NORTH WESTERN TRAINS
PO Box 44, Rail House, Store Street
Manchester M60 1DQ
Tel 0161 228 2141
Fax 0161 228 5003

REGIONAL RAILWAYS NORTH EAST
Main Headquarters Building, York YO1 1HT
Tel 01904 653022

SCOTRAIL RAILWAYS
Caledonian Chambers, 87 Union Street
Glasgow G1 3TA
Tel 0141 332 9811

SILVERLINK TRAIN SERVICES
65-67 Clarendon Raod, Watford WD1 1DP
Tel 01923 207258
Fax 01923 207023

SOUTH WEST TRAINS
Friars Bridge Court, 41-45 Blackfrairs Road
London SE1 8NZ
Tel 0171 928 5151
Fax 0171 902 3208

THAMESLINK RAIL
Friars Bridge, 41-45 Blackfriars Road,
London SE1 8NZ
Tel 0171 620 5760
Fax 0171 620 5099

THAMES TRAINS
Venture House, 37 Blagrave Street, Reading
RG1 1PZ
Tel 0118 908 3678
Fax 0118 957 9006

VIRGIN TRAINS
85 Smallbrook Queensway, Birmingham B5 4HA
Tel 0121 654 7400
Fax 0121 654 7487

WALES & WEST
Brunel House, 2 Fitzalan Rd, Cardiff CF2 1SU
Tel 01222 430400
Fax 01222 430214

WEST ANGLIA GREAT NORTHERN RAILWAY
Hertford House, 1 Cranwood Street, London
EC1V 9GT
Tel 0345 818919
Fax 01223 453606

WEST COAST RAILWAY COMPANY
Warton Road, Carnforth, Lancashire LA5 9HX
Tel 01524 732100
Fax 01524 735518

SOCCER RELATED INTERNET BOOKMARKS

The following three pages are a listing of soccer websites, some of which you may find useful to bookmark. As any internet browser will know all too well, URLs change, move or become obsolete at the drop of a hat. At the time of going to press all the ones listed were active.

If you are new to internet browsing, the following information on entering the URL addresses should be observed. Because of the way the address lines are printed, those longer than the width of the column are broken into two lines, the second slightly indented. Nevertheless, all the characters of the address should be typed in as one line, with no spaces between characters. If your edition or version of browser already enters the 'http://' characters, or does not require them, omit these from the URL address.

Where sites are official, it states so in brackets after the site name. Any useful notes about the site are given after the name in square brackets.

WORLD CUP RELATED PAGES

Football Web in Japan
http://www.nidnet.com/link/socweb.html
CBS SportsLine - Soccer
http://www.sportsline.com/u/soccer/index.html
Teams of the World
http://www.islandia.is/totw/
World Cup - Soccernet
http://www.soccernet.com/u/soccer/worldcup98/index.html
World Cup 1998 - CBS SportsLine
http://www.sportsline.com/u/soccer/worldcup98/qualifying/index.html
World Cup Soccer - France 98 - Coupe du Monde
http://www.worldcup.com/english/index.html

FOOTBALL RELATED

1997 edition of the Laws of the Game
http://www.fifa.com/fifa/handbook/laws/index.laws.html
Soccer Books [good reference]
http://www.soccer-books.co.uk
British Society of Sports History [reference material]
http://www.umist.ac.uk/UMIST_Sport/bssh.html
Buchanan Brigade Messge Bd Thirty-Three
http://www.buchanan.org/mb33.html
Communicata Football
http://www.communicata.co.uk/lookover/football/
Division 1 Web Pages [relates to the Nationwide leagues]
http://www.users.globalnet.co.uk/~emmas/ndiv1.htm
Division 2 Web Pages [old Endsleigh rather than the Nationwide]
http://www.uwm.edu/People/dyce/htfc/clubs/div2-www.html
England [Engerland]
http://www.users.dircon.co.uk/~england/england/
England [Green Flags England team pages]
http://www.greenflag.co.uk/te/fslist.html
England [English Soccernet - National Team - News]
http://www.soccernet.com/english/national/news/index.html
England
http://www.englandfc.com/
English Club Homepages
http://pluto.webbernet.net/~bob/engclub.html
FAI - Irish International
http://www.fai.ie/
GeordieSport!
http://www.geordiepride.demon.co.uk/geordiesport.htm
L & M Referees' Society - Soccer Pages
http://www.lancs.ac.uk/ug/williams/soccer.htm
Northern Ireland [Norn Iron!: The NI International Football 'zine]
http://students.un.umist.ac.uk/gbh/index.html
Notts Association
http://www.innotts.co.uk/~soccerstats/

gallery/nmf8.htm
Scotland [Rampant Scotland - Sport]
http://scotland.rampant.com/sport.htm
Scotland
http://web.cit}.ac.uk/~sh393/euro/scotland.htm
Scottish Football Association (Official)
http://www.scottishfa.co.uk/
Scottish Mailing Lists
http://www.isfa.com/isfa/lists/scotland.htm
Simply the Best
http://www.int-foot-fame.com/famers1.htm
Soccer ScoreSheet History List
http://www.kazmax.demon.co.uk/websheet/tm000309.htm
Soccer-Tables
http://www.marwin.ch/sport/fb/index.e.html
SoccerSearch: Players:G-P
http://www.soccersearch.com/Players/G-P/
SoccerSpace, Football & Soccer Links
http://www.winbet.sci.fi/soccerspace/links.htm
Team England - Fixtures & Results
http://ourworld.compuserve.com/homepages/nic_king/england/fixtures.htm
The Association of Football Statisticians
http://www.innotts.co.uk/~soccerstats/
The Aylesbury Branch of the Referees Association
http://homepages.bucks.net/~bigmick/
The Daily Soccer
http://www.dailysoccer.com/
The Football Supporters' Association (FSA)
http://www.fsa.org.uk/
US Soccer History Archives
http://www.sover.net/~spectrum/index.html
Welsh Football, Football wales, faw, welsh fa, ryan giggs
http://www.citypages.co.uk/faw/

ENGLISH PREMIERSHIP

Arsenal
http://www.arsenal.co.uk/
Aston Villa
http://www.geocities.com/Colosseum/Field/6089/
Aston Villa
http://www.villan.demon.co.uk/
Aston Villa
http://www.gbar.dtu.dk/~c937079/AVFC/index.html
Aston Villa (Official)
http://www.gbar.dtu.dk/~c937079/CB/
Barnsley
http://www.geocities.com/Colosseum/Field/6059/bfc.html
Barnsley
http://www.u-net.com/westex/bfc.htm
Barnsley
http://www.radders.skynet.co.uk/
Barnsley
http://upload.virgin.net/d.penty/Copacabarnsley/Copacabarnsley.htm
Barnsley
http://members.aol.com/JLister/bfc/bfc.htm
Blackburn Rovers
http://www.brfc-supporters.org.uk/
Blackburn Rovers (Official)
http://www.rovers.co.uk/
Bolton Wanderers
http://www.hankins.demon.co.uk/bwscl/index.html

Bolton Wanderers
http://www.netcomuk.co.uk/~cjw/football.html
Bolton Wanderers
http://www.geocities.com/Colosseum/4433/
Bolton Wanderers
http://mail.freeway.co.uk/druid/
Bolton Wanderers (Official)
http://www.boltonwfc.co.uk/
Charlton Athletic
http://www.demon.co.uk/casc/index.html
Chelsea
http://www.geocities.com/Colosseum/1457/chelsea.html
Chelsea
http://web.ukonline.co.uk/Members/jf.lettice/cfcmain.html
Chelsea
http://www.jack.dircon.net/chelsea/
Chelsea
http://fans-of.chelsea-fc.com/csr/
Chelsea FC (Official)
http://www.chelseafc.co.uk/chelsea/frontpage.shtml
Coventry City [mpegs of goals... that's it]
http://karpaty.tor.soliton.com/ccfcgoals/
Coventry City [The Sky Blue Superplex]
http://www.geocities.com/TimesSquare/Dungeon/1641/page4.html
Coventry City
http://www.warwick.ac.uk/~cudbu/SkyBlues.html
Coventry City (Official)
http://www.ccfc.co.uk/
Derby County
http://lard.sel.cam.ac.uk/derby_county/
Derby County
http://www.cheme.cornell.edu/~jwillits/this.html
Derby County
http://easyweb.easynet.co.uk/~nickwheat/ramsnet.html
Derby County
http://home.sol.no/~einasand/derby.htm
Derby County
http://www.cheme.cornell.edu/~jwillits/derby2.html#History
Derby County
http://www.derby-county.com/main.htm
Derby County (Official)
http://www.dcfc.co.uk/dcfc/index.html
Everton FC (Official)
http://www.connect.org.uk/everton/
Leeds United
http://www.lufc.co.uk/
Leeds United
http://spectrum.tcns.co.uk/cedar/leeds.htm
Leeds United
http://www.csc.liv.ac.uk/users/tim/Leeds/
Leeds United (Official - CarlingNet)
http://www.fa-premier.com/club/lufc/
Leicester City (Official)
http://www.lcfc.co.uk/141097b.htm
Liverpool
http://akureyri.ismennt.is/~jongeir/
Liverpool
http://www.soccernet.com/livrpool/
Liverpool
http://www.connect.org.uk/anfield/
Manchester United
http://www.cs.indiana.edu/hyplan/ccheah/posts.html
Manchester United
http://www.geocities.com/SouthBeach/6367

/index.html
Manchester United
http://www.sky.co.uk/sports/manu/
Manchester United
http://www.cybernet.dk/users/barrystorv/
Manchester United
http://home.pacific.net.sg/~jerping/
Manchester United
http://sunhehi.phy.uic.edu/~clive/MUFC/home.html
Manchester United
http://www.iol.ie/~mmurphy/red_devils/mufc.htm
Manchester United
http://www.davewest.demon.co.uk/
Manchester United
http://www.webcom.com/~solution/mufc/manu.html
Manchester United
http://ourworld.compuserve.com/homepages/red_devil/
Manchester United
http://xanadu.centrum.is/~runarhi/
Manchester United
http://web.city.ac.uk/~sh393/mufc.htm
Manchester United
http://www.wsu.edu:8080/~mmarks/Giggs.html
Manchester United
http://osiris.sunderland.ac.uk/online/access/manutd/redshome.html
Manchester United
http://www.u-net.com/~pitman/
Manchester United
http://www.geocities.com/Colosseum/2483/
Manchester United
http://www.wsu.edu:8080/~mmarks/mufclinks.html
Manchester United
http://gladstone.uoregon.edu:80/~jsetzen/mufc.html
Manchester United
http://members.hknet.com/~siukin/
Newcastle United
http://www.swan.co.uk/TOTT
Newcastle United
http://www.nufc.com
Newcastle United
http://www.btinternet.com/~the.magpie/history1.htm
Newcastle United
http://www.ccacyber.com/nufc/
Newcastle United
http://sunflower.singnet.com.sg/~resa21/
Nottingham Forest
http://users.homenet.ie/~aidanhut/
Nottingham Forest
http://www.thrustworld.co.uk/users/kryten/forest/
Nottingham Forest
http://hem1.passagen.se/pearce/index.htm
Nottingham Forest
http://www.innotts.co.uk/~joe90/forest.htm
Nottingham Forest
http://ourworld.compuserve.com/homepages/kencrossland/
Nottingham Forest (Official)
http://www.nottingham-forest.co.uk/frames.html
Sheffield Wednesday
http://www.crg.cs.nott.ac.uk/Users/anb/Football/stats/swfcarch.htm
Sheffield Wednesday
http://www.rhi.hi.is/~jbj/sheffwed/opnun.htm

BOOKMARKS

Sheffield Wednesday
http://www.geocities.com/Colosseum/2938/
Sheffield Wednesday
http://www.cs.nott.ac.uk/~anb/Football/
Southampton [Saintsweb]
http://www.soton.ac.uk/~saints/
Southampton [Marching In]
http://www.saintsfans.com/marchingin/
Tottenham Hotspur [White Hart Site]
http://www.xpress.se/~ssab0019/webring/
index.html
Tottenham Hotspur [Felix Gills' Page]
http://www.gilnet.demon.co.uk/spurs.htm
Tottenham Hotspur
http://www.personal.u-net.com/~spurs/
Tottenham Hotspur [check Spurs results
year-by-year - just stats]
http://www.bobexcell.demon.co.uk/
Tottenham Hotspur
http://www.btinternet.com/~matt.cook/
Tottenham Hotspur (Official)
http://www.spurs.co.uk/welcome.html
West Ham United
http://www.ecs.soton.ac.uk/saints/premier/
westham.htm
West Ham United
http://www.westhamunited.co.uk/
Wimbledon
http://www.fa-premier.com/cgi-bin/
fetch/club/wfc/home.html?team='WIM'
Wimbledon [unofficial - WISA]
http://www.wisa.org.uk/
Wimbledon [Womble.Net - Independent
Wimbledon FC Internet 'zine]
http://www.geocities.com/SunsetStrip/
Studio/6112/womblnet.html
Wimbledon [very basic]
http://www.aracnet.com/~davej/football.
htm
Wimbledon [unofficial - USA]
http://soyokaze.biosci.ohio-state.edu/~dcp/
wimbledon/womble.html
Wimbledon
http://www.city.ac.uk/~sh393/prem/
wimbeldon.htm
Wimbledon
http://www.netkonect.co.uk/b/brenford/
wimbledon/
Wimbledon [unofficial - WISA]
http://www.soi.city.ac.uk/homes/ec564/
donswisa.html
Wimbledon [John's Wimbledon FC page]
http://www.soi.city.ac.uk/homes/ec564/
dons.top.html
Wimbledon (Official)
http://www.wimbledon-fc.co.uk/

ENGLISH DIVISION 1

Birmingham City [PlanetBlues]
http://www.isfa.com/server/web/planetblues/
Birmingham City [BCFC Supports Club
Redditch Branch]
http://www.fortunecity.com/olympia/ovett/
135/
Birmingham City [Richy's B'ham City Page]
http://www.rshill.demon.co.uk/blues.htm
Bradford City
http://www.legend.co.uk/citygent/index.
html
Bury
http://www.brad.ac.uk/%7edjmartin/bury1.
html

Crystal Palace
http://www.gold.net/users/az21/cp_home.
htm
Fulham [The Independent Fulham Fans
Website: History]
http://www.fulhamfc.co.uk/History/history.
html
Fulham [FulhamWeb]
http://www.btinternet.com/~aredfern/
Fulham [Black & White Pages]
http://www.wilf.demon.co.uk/fulhamfc/ffc.
html
Fulham [unofficial - The Fulham Football
Club Mailing List]
http://www.users.dircon.co.uk/~troyj/
fulham/
Fulham
http://zeus.bris.ac.uk/~chmsl/fulham/
fulham.html
Fulham
http://www.netlondon.com/cgi-local/
wilma/spo.873399737.html
Fulham (Official) [mostly merchandising]
http://www.fulham-fc.co.uk/
Huddersfield Town
http://www.geocities.com/Colosseum/4401/
index.html
Huddersfield Town
http://ftp.csd.uwm.edu/People/dyce/htfc/
Huddersfield Town
http://granby.nott.ac.uk/~ppykara/htfc/
Huddersfield Town
http://www.uwm.edu:80/~dyce/htfc/index.
html
Ipswich Town [MATCHfacts - Datafile]
http://www.matchfacts.com/mfdclub/
ipswich.htm
Ipswich Town
http://www.sys.uea.ac.uk/Recreation/Sport/
itfc/
Ipswich Town [Those Were The Days]
http://www.twtd.co.uk/
Ipswich Town
http://members.wbs.net/homepages/a/d/a/
adamcable.html
Ipswich Town [The Online Portman Vista]
http://www.btinternet.com/~bluearmy/
index2.html
Ipswich Town [unofficial - Latest News -
not really]
http://www.rangey.demon.co.uk/ipswich.htm
Ipswich Town [IPSWICH TOWN tribute]
http://www.geocities.com/Colosseum/Track/
5399/
Ipswich Town [The Ipswich Town VRML Site
- techy, not much else]
http://www.sys.uea.ac.uk/Recreation/Sport/
itfc/vrml/vrml.html
Ipswich Town
http://homepages.enterprise.net/meo/itfc2.
html
Ipswich Town (Official)
http://www.itfc.co.uk/
Manchester City
http://www.uit.no/mancity/
Manchester City (Official)
http://www.mcfc.co.uk/
Middlesbrough
http://www.hk.super.net/~tlloyd/personal/
boro.html
Norwich City
http://ncfc.netcom.co.uk/ncfc/
Oxford United
http://www.aligrafix.co.uk/ag/fun/home/

OxTales/default.html
Oxford United
http://www.netlink.co.uk//users/oufc1/
index.html
Port Vale
http://www.netcentral.co.uk/~iglover/index.
html
Port Vale
http://web.dcs.hull.ac.uk/people/pjp/
PortVale/PortVale.html
Portsmouth [unofficial - History]
http://www.mech.port.ac.uk/StaffP/pb/
history.html
Portsmouth [Links page]
http://www.imsport.co.uk/imsport/ims/tt/
035/club.html
Queens Park Rangers
http://www-
dept.cs.ucl.ac.uk/students/M.Pemble/index.
html
Reading
http://www.i-way.co.uk/~readingfc/
Sheffield United
http://www.shef.ac.uk/city/blades/
Sheffield United
http://pine.shu.ac.uk/~cmssa/bifa.html
Sheffield United (Official)
http://www.sufc.co.uk/
Stoke City
http://www.cs.bham.ac.uk/~jdr/scfc/scfc.
htm
Sunderland (Official)
http://www.sunderland-afc.com/
Swindon Town
http://www.bath.ac.uk/~ee3cmk/swindon/
home.html
Tranmere Rovers
http://www.connect.org.uk/merseyworld/
tarantula/
Tranmere Rovers
http://www.brad.ac.uk/~mjhesp/tran.htm
West Bromwich Albion
http://pages.prodigy.com/FL/baggie/
West Bromwich Albion
http://www.gold.net/users/cp78/
West Bromwich Albion - Official
http://www.wba.co.uk/
Wolverhampton Wanderers [The Wandering
Wolf]
http://www.angelfire.com/wv/Quants/index.
html
Wolverhampton Wanderers
http://www.lazy-dog.demon.co.uk/wolves/
Wolverhampton Wanderers (Official)
http://www.idiscover.co.uk/wolves/

ENGLISH DIVISION 2

AFC Bournemouth
http://www.bath.ac.uk/~ee6dlah/club.htm
AFC Bournemouth
http://www.homeusers.prestel.co.uk/rose220
/afcb1.htm
AFC Bournemouth
http://www.maths.soton.ac.uk/rpb/AFCB.
html
AFC Bournemouth
http://www.maths.soton.ac.uk/rpb/AFCB.
html
AFC Bournemouth
http://www.geocities.com/TimesSquare/
Arcade/7499/afcb.htm
AFC Bournemouth (Official)
http://www.afcb.co.uk/

Blackpool
http://web.ukonline.co.uk/Members/
c.moffat/basil/
Bristol City
http://ourworld.compuserve.com/homepages
/redrobins/
Bristol Rovers
http://dialspace.dial.pipex.com/town/street
/xko88/
Bristol Rovers
http://members.wbs.net/homepages/l/a/r/
lardon/
Bristol Rovers
http://www.cf.ac.uk/uwcc/engin/brittonr/
rovers/index.html
Bristol Rovers
http://www.geocities.com/Colosseum/6542/
Bristol Rovers
http://www.personal.unet.com/~coley/
rovers/
Bristol Rovers
http://www.btinternet.com/~uk/BRFC/
Bristol Rovers
http://www.btinternet.com/~uk/
BristolRovers/index.html
Bristol Rovers
http://www.cowan.edu.au/~gprewett/gas.
htm
Bristol Rovers
http://www.cf.ac.uk/uwcc/engin/brittonr/
rovers/index.html
Burnley
http://www.zensys.co.uk/home/page/trevor.
ent/
Burnley
http://www.theturf.demon.co.uk/burnley.
htm
Burnley
http://www.zen.co.uk/home/page/p.bassek/
Burnley
http://www.mtattersall.demon.co.uk/index.
html
Burnley
http://home.sol.no/~parald/burnley/
Burnley
http://www.geocities.com/Colosseum/7075/
index.html
Carlisle United
http://www.aston.ac.uk/~jonespm/
Carlisle United
http://dspace.dial.pipex.com/town/square/
ad969/
Chester City [Silly Sausage - good history]
http://www.sillysausage.demon.co.uk/
history.htm
Chester City (Official)
http://www.chester-city.co.uk/
Gillingham
http://ourworld.compuserve.com/homepages
/gillsf.c/
Grimsby Town
http://www.aston.ac.uk/~etherina/index.
Preston North End [unofficial - PNEWeb
HomePage]
http://freespace.virgin.net/paul.billington
/PNEWeb_homepage.html
Preston North End [unofficial - PNE Pages]
http://www.dpne.demon.co.uk/pages/
pagesf.html
Preston North End [pie muncher online -
front door]
http://www.pylonvu.demon.co.uk/pm/pm.
html

BOOKMARKS

Swansea City
http://www2.prestel.co.uk/gmartin/index.
html
Wrexham
http://www.aber.ac.uk/~deg/wxm/text.html
Wrexham
http://www.csm.uwe.ac.uk/~klhender/wxm/
index.html
Wycombe Wanderers
http://ourworld.compuserve.com/homepages
/chairboys/

ENGLISH DIVISION 3

Brighton and Hove Albion
http://www.bmharding.demon.co.uk/
seagulls/index.html/
Brighton and Hove Albion
http://homepages.enterprise.net/gjc/
Brighton and Hove Albion
http://www.aber.ac.uk/~bmh1/seagulls/
Cardiff City (Official)
http://www.styrotech.co.uk/ccafc/
Cardiff City
http://www.cf.ac.uk/uwcm/mg/bloo/biz.
html
Cardiff City
http://www.geocities.com/Colosseum/1943/
Cardiff City
http://ds.dial.pipex.com/m4morris/ccafc.
htm
Chester City
http://www.sillysausage.demon.co.uk/others
.htm
Halifax Town
http://www.geocities.com/Colosseum/
Stadium/3043/
Halifax Town [Aussie Style]
http://expage.com/page/Shaymen
Halifax Town [Shaymen]
http://www.shaymen.clara.net/shaymen.html
Hull City
http://www.demon.co.uk/Vox/hullcity/
hullcity.html
Hull City
http://www.hullcity.demon.co.uk/
Leyton Orient (Official -OriNet)

http://www.matchroom.com/orient/
Leyton Orient [WebOrient - Global Orient
Website]
http://www.web-orient.clara.net/
Macclesfield Town
http://www.cs.man.ac.uk/~griffitm/
macctown/
Mansfield Town
http://www.footballnews.co.uk/clubs/1068/
home.htm
Notts County
http://home.sol.no/~benn/magpienet/
Notts County
http://www.nbs.ntu.ac.uk/Staff/baylidj/
ncfc.htm
Notts County
http://www.nbs.ntu.ac.uk/Staff/baylidj/
ncfc.htm
Notts County
http://www.athene.net/soccercity/europe/e
ng/nc.htm
Notts County
http://www.imsport.co.uk/imsport/ims/tt/
032/032.html
Scunthorpe United [The Iron Network]
http://www.fortunecity.com/wembley/villa/
56/index.html
Scunthorpe United [Mailing List]
http://www.isfa.com/isfa/lists/scunthorpe/
Scunthorpe United [Iron World]
http://freespace.virgin.net/su.fc/
Shrewsbury Town
http://www.netlink.co.uk/users/ian/shrews/
shrews.html
Shrewsbury Town
http://www.shrewsburytown.co.uk/
Swansea City
http://homepages.enterprise.net/gmartin/
Swansea City
http://homepages.enterprise.net/gmartin/
indexnf.html

SCOTTISH PREMIER LEAGUE

Aberdeen - Official
http://www.afc.co.uk/site/

Aberdeen
http://homepages.enterprise.net/howburn/
Aberdeen
http://www.web13.co.uk/dons/
Aberdeen
http://www.raik.grid9.net/dons/
Aberdeen
http://www.raik.demon.co.uk/dons/
Aberdeen
http://freespace.virgin.net/a.morrison/ajm/
afchome2.htm
Celtic (Official)
http://www.celticfc.co.uk/presecurity2.html
Celtic
http://www.erols.com/gbrown/dccelts.htm
Celtic
http://www.presence.co.uk/soccer/pages/
history.html
Dundee United
http://www.algonet.se/~snoe/dfc/
Dundee United
http://www.arabland.demon.co.uk/news.htm
Dunfermline Athletic
http://www.webadvertising.co.uk/wwwboard
/pars2/
Dunfermline Athletic [Soccernet]
http://www.soccernet.com/scottish/dafc/
index.html
Dunfermline Athletic
http://www.aiai.ed.ac.uk/~wth/dunfermline/
dunfermline.html
Heart of Midlothian (Official)
http://www.heartsfc.co.uk/
Heart of Midlothian [No Idle Talk - okay]
http://web.ukonline.co.uk/Members/grant.
thorburn/nit1.htm
Heart of Midlothian
http://jambos.aurdev.com/update.html
Heart of Midlothian [has a squad list. USA]
http://www.geocities.com/Colosseum/Arena/
2659/
Heart of Midlothian [Electronic Jam Tart]
http://www.ednet.co.uk/~ricw/
Heart of Midlothian [M'chester Hearts fans]
http://www.rigor.demon.co.uk/manheart.htm
Heart of Midlothian [OrwellHeartsSC]
http://members.aol.com/orwellhsc/

orwellhearts/index.html
Heart of Midlothian [Midlands Hearts]
http://members.aol.com/gsha27/
midlandhearts1.htm
Heart of Midlothian [Hearts Supporters USA
- not very informative]
http://jambos.aurdev.com/
Heart of Midlothian [Always The Bridesmaid]
http://ourworld.compuserve.com/homepages
/a_macdougall_and_ATB/
Heart of Midlothian [Rainbow Hearts S.C.
Homepage]
http://ourworld.compuserve.com/homepages
/andy_rainbow_hearts/
Kilmarnock
http://homepages.enterprise.net/wallace/
Kilmarnock
http://www.enterprise.net/kilmarnockfc/
index.htm
Motherwell
http://www.isfa.com/server/web/
motherwell/
Rangers (Official) [you need to register]
http://www.rangers.co.uk/channels/
Rangers
http>//www.ukfootballpages.com/rangers/
Rangers
http://www.cee.hw.ac.uk/~johnc/Rangers/
homepage.html
Rangers
http://www.geocities.com/Tokyo/Flats/
5554/home.html
Rangers
http://www.geocities.com/Colosseum/Field/
2968/
Rangers
http://dspace.dial.pipex.com/x-static/
rangers.htm
Rangers
http://www.sgwoozy.force9.co.uk/rangers.
html
Rangers
http://www.geocities.com/Colosseum/Track/
7990/
Rangers
http://members.aol.com/broxinet/index.
html

WEBSITE NOTES

WIN A FREE FOOTBALL BOOK!

Thank-you for buying a copy of our soccer yearbooks, covering all teams in the English Premiership, Scottish Premiership, and English Divisions 1, 2 and 3. We hope that you are happy with your purchase.

This unique collection of yearbooks, gives each supporter in the land their own club diary, supported by all-action shots from the greatest highlights of the last season, plus a diary from July 1998 – June 1999, detailing all club fixtures for the season.

If you would like to be kept informed of other football titles and next season's yearbooks, please cut out and complete this form and mail it back to me: Sharon Pitcher – Marketing Manager, Parragon, 13 Whiteladies Road, Bristol, BS8 1PB. Ten Lucky respondents will receive a free football book for their trouble!

Name of Favourite
Team(s) . . . .
. . . .

Name of Local
Team(s) . . . .
. . . .

Where did you
buy this book? . . . .

Your Name: . . . .

Street: . . . .

Town: . . . .

County: . . . .

Postcode: . . . .

Email: . . . .

❏ Yes – please keep me informed of other football titles, plus next season's football yearbooks.
This information is being collected on behalf of Parragon Book Services Ltd.

For office use only